CW00816041

Smart Government: Practical Uses for Artificial Intelligence in Local Government

1, Volume 1

Chris Chiancone

Published by Chris Chiancone, 2023.

While every precaution has been taken in the preparation of this book, the publisher assumes no responsibility for errors or omissions, or for damages resulting from the use of the information contained herein.

SMART GOVERNMENT: PRACTICAL USES FOR ARTIFICIAL INTELLIGENCE IN LOCAL GOVERNMENT

First edition. April 20, 2023.

ISBN: 979-8223652984

Written by Chris Chiancone.

Table of Contents

Dedication

Dedication

To my invaluable mentors, Jim Parrish, Curle Matthews, and Bruce Glasscock, who have guided and inspired me throughout this journey; your wisdom and unwavering support have been my guiding light.

To my loving wife, Bernadette, my rock and my constant source of strength, encouragement, and love; without you, this journey would have been incomplete.

To my children, Rachel, Jake, Tori, and Nick, who have filled my life with joy and purpose; may you always be inspired to chase your dreams and embrace the endless possibilities the world has to offer.

To my parents, for their unconditional love, support, and the strong foundation they have provided me, both personally and professionally; I am forever grateful.

And finally, to my dedicated staff and friends, whose passion, commitment, and hard work have been instrumental in bringing this project to life; you have made an indelible impact, and I am truly grateful for each one of you.

This book is dedicated to all of you, with love and gratitude.

Smart Government: Practical Uses for Artificial Intelligence in Local Government

Introduction

Artificial Intelligence (AI) is rapidly transforming the world we live in, and its impact on government is no exception. As cities become smarter, local governments have a unique opportunity to harness the power of AI to improve efficiency, reduce costs, and enhance services for their citizens. The adoption of AI can revolutionize the way local governments operate and provide services to their citizens.

By leveraging AI, local governments can streamline their processes and reduce the time and resources required to carry out various tasks. This can lead to significant cost savings, allowing governments to allocate resources to other areas and initiatives that benefit citizens. For example, AI-powered systems for building maintenance and repair can help reduce costs and improve the quality of public housing for citizens. Similarly, AI-powered traffic management systems can reduce congestion, improve transportation efficiency, and enhance the overall transportation experience for citizens.

The use of AI can also lead to improved citizen services and greater citizen engagement. Chatbots powered by AI can help governments provide more personalized and efficient services to citizens, while also freeing up staff to focus on more complex tasks. This can lead to greater citizen satisfaction and trust in their local government. AI-powered platforms for citizen feedback and engagement can also help local governments better understand the needs and preferences of their citizens, allowing them to make more informed policy decisions.

Furthermore, the adoption of AI can create new opportunities for innovation and economic growth in local communities. As local governments embrace the power of AI, they can attract new businesses and startups that specialize in AI technologies and applications. This can create new job opportunities and help local economies thrive.

However, there are also challenges associated with the adoption of AI in local government. These include concerns over privacy and data security, as well as the need for specialized skills and expertise to develop and implement AI-powered systems. Local governments must carefully consider these challenges and work to address them to fully realize the benefits of AI.

In this book, we will delve into the practical uses of AI in local government and explore how it can be harnessed to improve the lives of citizens. From enhancing public safety to streamlining procurement processes, AI offers local governments a wide range of opportunities to optimize their operations and enhance the services they provide to citizens.

Each chapter in this book will focus on a specific use case for AI in local government, providing detailed information on how it works, the benefits it can offer, and examples of its successful implementation. Readers will gain insights into the ways that AI-powered systems can improve public safety, reduce traffic congestion, enhance citizen services, and much more.

For instance, in the chapter on enhancing public safety with AI, readers will learn about the use of predictive analytics and facial recognition technology to identify high-risk areas and individuals, as well as the use of AI-powered drones for search and rescue operations. They will also discover how AI can be used to optimize traffic flow and reduce congestion in the chapter on improving traffic flow with AI.

Through real-world examples and detailed explanations of how AI-powered systems work, readers will gain a comprehensive understanding of the practical applications of AI in local government. They will see how AI can be used to create smarter, more efficient, and more responsive communities, and how it can improve the lives of citizens in meaningful ways.

By the end of this book, readers will have a clear understanding of the many opportunities that AI offers to local governments. They will be equipped with the knowledge and insights they need to effectively implement AI-powered systems in their own communities, and to drive positive change for their citizens.

This book is a must-read for anyone interested in the practical applications of AI in local government. It provides a comprehensive overview of the many ways that AI can be used to improve the lives of citizens and offers detailed insights into the benefits it can offer. By exploring specific use cases and providing examples of successful implementation, this book will inspire readers to explore the possibilities of AI and drive positive change in their own communities.

Chapter 1: Enhancing Public Safety with AI

The safety of citizens is a top priority for local governments, and AI can play a vital role in enhancing public safety in local communities. In this chapter, we will explore how AI-powered systems can be used to identify high-risk areas and individuals, assist with criminal investigations, and provide critical support for search and rescue operations, disaster response, and traffic management.

One of the most exciting and potentially transformative applications of AI in public safety is the use of predictive analytics. By analyzing large amounts of data, AI-powered systems can identify patterns and trends that may be indicative of criminal activity. This can help law enforcement agencies to proactively address potential threats and prevent crime before it occurs. The power of predictive analytics lies in its ability to identify risks that might otherwise go unnoticed, enabling law enforcement to focus their resources on the areas where they are most needed.

AI-powered predictive analytics can be used to identify high-risk areas and individuals in a variety of ways. For example, by analyzing crime data from across a city, AI-powered systems can identify patterns and trends that may be indicative of criminal activity. This can help law enforcement to proactively address potential threats and prevent crime before it occurs. For instance, if a particular neighborhood experiences a high number of burglaries during a certain time of day, AI-powered predictive analytics can identify the pattern and alert law enforcement agencies to increase patrols in the area during those hours.

Similarly, predictive analytics can be used to identify individuals who may be at risk of committing a crime. By analyzing a wide range of data, including criminal records, social media activity, and other public data sources, AI-powered systems can identify individuals who may be more likely to engage in criminal activity. This can help law enforcement agencies to intervene before a crime is committed and prevent potential harm to individuals or the community.

The benefits of AI-powered predictive analytics in public safety are clear. By enabling law enforcement agencies to identify high-risk areas and individuals, they can focus their resources on the areas where they are most needed. This can lead to more efficient use of resources and a reduction in crime rates. Furthermore, predictive analytics can help to improve community relations by focusing law enforcement efforts on areas that need the most attention, while reducing the need for broad-based and potentially discriminatory policing strategies.

Local governments across the world are embracing the power of predictive analytics to enhance public safety in their communities. Predictive analytics, coupled with AI and machine learning, enables local governments to predict and anticipate potential issues before they escalate into crises. This section will provide real-world examples of local governments using predictive analytics to enhance public safety in their communities, as gathered from the provided web search results.

One example of predictive analytics in government is the Strategic Subjects List (SSL) system implemented by the Chicago Police Department. The SSL system uses data analysis to identify high-risk individuals who may be at risk of becoming involved in violent crimes, either as perpetrators or victims. By proactively identifying these individuals and intervening before a crime is committed, the Chicago Police Department has been able to reduce the number of shootings and homicides in some of the city's most violent neighborhoods.

Another example is the PredPol system implemented by the Los Angeles Police Department. PredPol uses predictive analytics to identify high-risk areas for property crime, allowing the police department to deploy officers to those areas proactively. As a result, PredPol has led to a significant reduction in burglaries in areas where it was implemented.

In the United Kingdom, the Metropolitan Police Service in London implemented a system called the Gangs Matrix. The system uses predictive analytics to identify and track individuals involved in gang activity and predict potential gang-related violence. While the system has been controversial due to privacy and racial profiling concerns, the Metropolitan Police Service has defended its use as an effective tool for preventing gang-related violence.

Predictive analytics can also be used for non-violent crimes, such as traffic management. The city of Los Angeles uses an AI-powered traffic management system to analyze traffic data and predict traffic patterns, allowing the city to adjust traffic signals proactively and reduce traffic congestion. Similarly, the city of Las Vegas uses a predictive analytics system to predict maintenance needs for city vehicles, allowing for more efficient scheduling of maintenance and reducing downtime.

In Australia, the government of New South Wales implemented a predictive analytics system to identify children who are at risk of being removed from their homes due to abuse or neglect. The system uses data from multiple sources, including healthcare records, to identify risk factors and intervene proactively to support families and prevent children from being removed from their homes.

These real-world examples demonstrate the power of predictive analytics in enhancing public safety in local communities. By proactively identifying potential risks and intervening before issues escalate, local governments can create safer, more efficient, and more responsive communities that benefit all citizens. As local governments continue to embrace the power of AI and predictive analytics, we can expect to see more innovative and effective solutions to public safety challenges.

Facial recognition technology is rapidly advancing and becoming a powerful tool for enhancing public safety. This technology can be used to compare images of individuals quickly and accurately against databases of known criminals, enabling law enforcement agencies to identify suspects and assist with criminal investigations.

The potential benefits of facial recognition technology in public safety are clear. In fact, this technology has already been used successfully in several high-profile cases, leading to the apprehension of dangerous criminals, and helping to keep communities safe. For instance, law enforcement agencies have used facial recognition technology to identify and apprehend suspects in cases involving terrorism, violent crime, and child exploitation.

However, there are also valid concerns about the use of facial recognition technology in public safety. One of the biggest concerns is the potential for privacy violations and misuse of personal information. In fact, some companies have faced class-action lawsuits for violating privacy laws by using facial recognition technology without proper consent.

To address these concerns, responsible use principles and legislative frameworks are being developed to ensure that facial recognition technology is used appropriately and in a manner that protects citizens' privacy rights. For example, the European Union has enacted strict regulations governing the use of facial recognition technology, while the U.S. government is currently exploring regulatory frameworks to ensure its responsible use.

While facial recognition technology has been a topic of controversy, there are examples of local governments utilizing this tool for public safety purposes. However, it is important to note that the use of facial recognition technology by law enforcement agencies has been the subject of ongoing debate regarding privacy concerns and potential misuse.

As of January 2022, some cities in the United States are backing off from previous attempts to ban facial recognition technology, despite concerns regarding privacy and surveillance. Additionally, there have been reports of federal agencies planning to increase their use of facial recognition technology in the aftermath of the racial justice protests in 2020 and the attack on the U.S. Capitol in January 2021.

The Government Accountability Office (GAO) discovered that approximately half of the federal agencies that employ law enforcement officers use facial recognition technology. For example, an agency plans to pilot the use of facial recognition technology to automate the identity verification process for travelers at airports.

In contrast, several states have implemented laws limiting the use of facial recognition technology by law enforcement, such as California and Oregon. Additionally, activist groups such as the Electronic Frontier Foundation have advocated for a complete ban on the use of facial recognition technology by government agencies, citing concerns about privacy, free expression, and social justice.

While facial recognition technology can be a powerful tool for law enforcement in criminal investigations, it is essential to balance public safety concerns with privacy concerns and potential misuse. Local governments should carefully evaluate the use of facial recognition technology and consider implementing measures to safeguard individual rights and privacy.

Some countries have implemented stricter regulations and limitations on the use of facial recognition technology. For example, the European Union has introduced the General Data Protection Regulation (GDPR), which imposes stringent requirements on the collection, processing, and storage of personal data, including biometric data such as facial images. In Canada, facial recognition technology is subject to the Personal Information Protection and Electronic Documents Act (PIPEDA), which governs the collection, use, and disclosure of personal information.

Moreover, some countries have taken a more cautious approach to facial recognition technology. For instance, in the United Kingdom, a parliamentary committee called for a moratorium on the use of facial recognition technology by the police until adequate legal safeguards are in place. In Australia, the government has introduced a set of voluntary privacy guidelines for the use of facial recognition technology by private companies.

While facial recognition technology has become ubiquitous in many countries, the approaches to its regulation and deployment vary widely. The United States has seen a proliferation of the technology, particularly in law enforcement, with a lack of federal regulation resulting in unchecked use and potential abuses. In contrast, some countries have implemented stricter regulations and limitations on the use of facial recognition technology, while others have taken a more cautious approach. It is crucial to strike a balance between the potential benefits and the risks and harms of facial recognition technology to ensure its responsible use and protect the privacy and civil liberties of individuals.

The use of AI-powered drones is revolutionizing various industries, and the applications for search and rescue operations, disaster response, and traffic management are numerous. Equipped with cameras and other sensors, drones can survey areas that may be difficult for humans to access, making them invaluable in emergency situations where time is critical.

Drones can provide real-time footage of disaster-stricken areas, allowing first responders to identify the location of survivors and coordinate rescue efforts effectively. Furthermore, AI algorithms can analyze the data gathered by drones, providing valuable insights into the conditions of the affected area. For example, AI-powered drones can be used to detect hotspots during wildfires or monitor the spread of hazardous materials.

Traffic management is another area where AI-powered drones can be useful. They can quickly survey the area and analyze traffic patterns, identifying bottlenecks and congested areas. This data can then be used to optimize traffic flow and reduce congestion.

Moreover, AI-powered drones can be used for traffic management, helping to reduce congestion and improve the overall flow of traffic. By analyzing traffic patterns and identifying potential bottlenecks, AI-powered systems can adjust traffic signals and other infrastructure in real-time to optimize traffic flow and reduce congestion.

Local governments are increasingly turning to drones as a cost-effective tool for a variety of applications. From surveying homeless encampments in wooded areas to inspecting infrastructure and assisting in hazardous materials responses, drones are proving to be an asset for local governments.

For instance, Pierce County, Washington has banned county departments from using drones to gather evidence related to criminal investigations. Meanwhile, the Interior Department has used drones in 25 different mission areas, including scientific research, surveillance, and search and rescue.

Drones have also been used by local hazardous materials teams in response to incidents in South Texas, allowing for real-time imagery and enhanced situational awareness. Additionally, local governments can use drones for cost-effective surveying and inspection of infrastructure, saving time and reducing the risks associated with human inspection.

Furthermore, drones can help local governments work smarter and make more efficient use of resources while enhancing health and safety. They can be used to monitor traffic, survey disaster-stricken areas, and enhance law enforcement, among other applications. For example, the Seattle Police Department initially purchased two drones for enhanced situational awareness at both the command and operations level.

Overall, drones have the potential to enhance local governments' services, deliver savings, and streamline their operations. As such, more and more local governments are exploring the benefits of drones and investing in them to improve their services and achieve their goals.

Some more recent uses of drone technology continue to advance, local governments are finding innovative ways to incorporate drones into their daily operations. Here are some examples of how local governments are using drones in 2023:

1. Law Enforcement and Search and Rescue: Several local law enforcement agencies are using drones equipped with thermal imaging technology to assist with search and rescue missions. Drones are also being used to track down fugitives evading arrest.
2. Infrastructure Inspection: Drones are being used to inspect bridges, tunnels, and other critical infrastructure. This not only saves time but also improves safety for inspectors who would otherwise have to work at great heights or in other dangerous conditions.
3. Disaster Response: Drones are playing an increasingly important role in disaster response efforts. They can be used to survey damage from natural disasters, assess the safety of structures, and locate missing persons.
4. Medical Supply Delivery: Drones are being used to deliver medical supplies to remote or hard-to-reach areas. This can be especially useful in emergency situations where time is of the essence.
5. Environmental Monitoring: Drones are being used to monitor environmental conditions and wildlife populations in local parks and other natural areas.

Overall, the benefits of drones in local government are clear. They can help to increase efficiency, improve safety, and save time and money. As drone technology continues to improve, we can expect to see even more innovative uses of drones in local government in the years to come.

Chapter 2: Improving Traffic Flow with AI

Traffic congestion is a widespread problem in many cities around the world, leading to a range of negative consequences, including lost productivity, increased pollution, and frustrated citizens. With more people moving into cities every day, the issue of traffic congestion is becoming more severe. To address this problem, governments and transportation planners are turning to emerging technologies, including artificial intelligence (AI), to help optimize traffic flow, reduce congestion, and improve public transportation.

In this chapter, we will explore how AI can be used to improve traffic flow, reduce congestion, and enhance public transportation. We will discuss the use of AI-powered traffic management systems, smart traffic lights, and predictive analytics to optimize the flow of traffic and improve the overall transportation experience for citizens.

AI-Powered Traffic Management Systems

AI-powered traffic management systems are designed to analyze real-time traffic data to optimize traffic flow and reduce congestion. These systems use a range of technologies, including sensors, cameras, and machine learning algorithms, to collect and analyze data on traffic patterns, road conditions, and other factors that affect traffic flow.

One of the most pressing issues facing modern cities is traffic congestion. This issue leads to a loss in productivity, increased pollution, and frustrated citizens. Fortunately, modern technologies, such as artificial intelligence (AI), are being used to tackle this problem. One such example is the Urban Traffic Control (UTC) system in Singapore, which is an AI-powered traffic management system that uses data from GPS devices, cameras, and road sensors to monitor traffic flow and adjust traffic signals in real-time.

The UTC system's use of AI algorithms to predict traffic patterns and adjust signal timings accordingly is the key to its success in reducing congestion and improving traffic flow. By analyzing vast amounts of data from various sources, the system can accurately predict traffic patterns and adjust signal timings to match the flow of traffic. This, in turn, reduces congestion and helps to keep traffic moving efficiently.

Moreover, the UTC system's use of AI algorithms is not limited to the prediction of traffic patterns. It also includes the ability to make decisions about how to allocate resources in real-time. The system can analyze the data it collects and use it to make decisions about which areas of the city need more resources to improve traffic flow. This dynamic allocation of resources allows the system to adjust to changes in traffic patterns and ensures that the system remains effective even as conditions change.

Another key feature of the UTC system is its ability to integrate with other transportation systems. For example, the system can work with public transportation systems to optimize the timing of buses and trains, reducing wait times and improving the overall efficiency of the transportation network. This integration of different systems is crucial to ensuring that the entire transportation network works together seamlessly to reduce congestion and improve traffic flow.

Smart Traffic Lights

Smart traffic lights are revolutionizing the way traffic flows through our cities. With the help of AI algorithms and advanced sensors, smart traffic lights can monitor traffic patterns and adjust signal timings in real-time, reducing congestion and improving the overall transportation experience for citizens. These lights are not just a concept, as there are several projects already underway to implement them in different cities around the world.

One such project is being developed by Damon Wischik at Cambridge University, where he is using AI to develop software to control traffic signals in UK cities. His software uses data from various sources such as cameras, GPS devices, and road sensors to monitor traffic flow and adjust signal timings accordingly. This optimization can reduce congestion and improve the flow of traffic.

Smart traffic lights are also being developed by startups that use sensors, cameras, and AI to enable more efficient vehicle flow through intersections, potentially coordinating with vehicle automation. These lights look the same as regular traffic lights but have extra hardware elements such as IoT sensors to enable smart operation.

Smart traffic lights can detect patterns of traffic and the volume of vehicles, pedestrians, and bicyclists approaching an intersection, making them dynamic and responsive to real-time traffic conditions. By adjusting signal timings in real-time, they can help move traffic through the city more efficiently, reduce wait times at intersections, and make traffic flow more smoothly.

These lights are not just a futuristic concept but are already being implemented in various cities worldwide. Siemens Mobility has built a prototype monitoring system in Bengaluru, India, that uses data from sensors to detect traffic patterns and adjust signal timings accordingly. Adaptive road traffic control systems that use AI to optimize the flow of vehicles through an urban area have also been developed and implemented in some cities, reducing waiting time at traffic lights by up to half.

Smart traffic lights are not just about reducing congestion, but also improving safety. Traffic jams increase the frequency of people running red lights out of frustration. By optimizing the flow of traffic in real-time, smart traffic lights can potentially reduce the number of drivers driving through a red light by up to 80%.

The use of smart traffic light systems like SCOOT in London has revolutionized the way we manage traffic flow in urban areas. These systems use real-time data from sensors, cameras, and GPS devices to adjust signal timings, reducing congestion and improving travel times for motorists. With smart traffic lights, drivers can expect to spend less time idling at intersections and more time moving through the city. Additionally, the reduction of idling cars can lead to a significant decrease in greenhouse gas emissions, making these systems not only more efficient but also more environmentally friendly.

The SCOOT system specifically has been shown to reduce journey times by up to 12% during peak hours, making commutes faster and more efficient for drivers. This is accomplished by using real-time data on traffic flow to adjust signal timings, allowing for smoother and more efficient movement of vehicles through intersections. And SCOOT is not the only system available: there are a variety of smart traffic light systems out there that utilize different technologies and methodologies to achieve the same goals of reducing congestion and improving traffic flow.

Overall, the benefits of smart traffic light systems are numerous and significant. They can make commutes faster, safer, and more enjoyable for drivers, reduce emissions, and improve overall traffic flow in urban areas. As cities continue to grow and traffic becomes an even bigger issue, these systems will become increasingly important in keeping our roads running smoothly and efficiently.

Predictive Analytics

Predictive analytics is a powerful technology that can revolutionize the transportation industry, particularly in traffic flow and congestion reduction. Predictive analytics algorithms use historical data on traffic patterns to predict future traffic conditions, enabling transportation planners to make proactive decisions to reduce congestion and improve traffic flow.

Predictive analytics can be conducted manually or using machine-learning algorithms. Regression analysis, for example, can determine the relationship between two or more variables and is a key predictive analytics tool. With regression analysis, transportation planners can analyze traffic data to identify patterns, extrapolate hidden trends, and predict future traffic conditions.

By leveraging the power of predictive analytics, transportation planners can identify traffic hotspots and anticipate traffic congestion before it occurs. This can lead to more efficient traffic management and reduced congestion, as transportation planners can make proactive decisions to redirect traffic or adjust signal timings to avoid bottlenecks.

Some of the top predictive analytics software platforms and solutions available today include Alteryx Analytics Automation Platform, Amazon SageMaker, H20 AI Cloud, IBM SPSS, RapidMiner, and SAP Analytics Cloud. These tools can help transportation planners to process large amounts of data and extract valuable insights that can inform decisions on how to optimize traffic flow and reduce congestion.

Predictive analytics can also be used for delivery optimization, ensuring on-time deliveries even when unexpected events occur. By predicting traffic congestion and other events that can impact delivery times, transportation planners can optimize trucking routes and improve delivery efficiency.

In addition to delivery optimization, predictive analytics can also be used in marketing to acquire new customers, retain existing customers, and maximize sales. Look-alike modeling is one key use case for predictive analytics in marketing, helping to identify potential customers who share characteristics with existing customers and are therefore more likely to convert.

With predictive analytics, transportation planners can make data-driven decisions to optimize traffic flow and reduce congestion, leading to a more efficient and sustainable transportation system. Descriptive, predictive, prescriptive, and diagnostic analytics are the four types of data analytics that give transportation planners the tools to understand what happened, what could happen next, what should happen in the future, and why something happened in the past. Predictive analytics is a powerful tool that enables transportation planners to predict and anticipate future traffic conditions, leading to more efficient and effective transportation management and reduced congestion.

The market for predictive analytics is projected to hit $10.5 billion this year and is expected to nearly triple in size to $28 billion by 2026, according to Markets and Markets. The rapid growth of the predictive analytics market underscores the importance of this technology in today's data-driven world and highlights the potential impact it can have in improving traffic flow and reducing congestion.

One example of predictive analytics in action is the Smart Traveler program in Los Angeles is a prime example of how predictive analytics can be used to improve traffic flow and reduce congestion. By using historical data on traffic patterns, road closures, and other factors, the program predicts future traffic conditions and provides real-time information to motorists. With this information, motorists can make informed decisions about their travel plans and avoid congested areas, leading to reduced congestion and smoother traffic flow.

The benefits of the Smart Traveler program extend beyond just reducing congestion. By providing real-time information to motorists, the program also improves safety by alerting drivers to potential hazards and accidents. Additionally, the program can improve air quality by reducing the time that vehicles spend idling in traffic, which can help to reduce pollution.

This example demonstrates the versatility and usefulness of predictive analytics in a real-world setting. From finance to sports to retail, predictive analytics is being used to make data-driven decisions and improve outcomes. As the market for predictive analytics continues to grow, more organizations are discovering the benefits of using historical data and statistical modeling to make predictions about future outcomes.

Enhancing Public Transportation

Artificial intelligence (AI) is a transformative technology that can bring a range of benefits to public transportation, reducing reliance on private vehicles, and ultimately decreasing traffic congestion. By providing real-time information on public transportation options, AI-powered transportation systems can encourage more people to use public transportation and reduce the number of cars on the road. In this three-page document, we will explore how AI can be used to enhance public transportation and reduce traffic congestion.

First, AI can be used to provide real-time information on public transportation options. By analyzing real-time traffic data and public transportation schedules, AI-powered transportation systems can provide accurate and up-to-date information on the availability of public transportation options. This can include the current location of buses and trains, estimated arrival times, and any delays or service disruptions. By providing this information to commuters, AI can help them make informed decisions about their transportation options, reducing wait times and improving the overall commuting experience.

One excellent example of AI-powered transportation systems in action is the Singapore Mass Rapid Transit (MRT) system. The system uses a combination of real-time data and predictive algorithms to optimize the frequency of trains and predict the arrival times of trains with high accuracy. This has significantly reduced waiting times for commuters, making the MRT system one of the most reliable public transportation systems globally.

Second, AI can be used to optimize public transportation routes and schedules. By analyzing data on passenger volume and traffic patterns, AI can identify the most efficient routes and schedules for buses and trains. This can help reduce wait times and improve the overall reliability of public transportation, making it a more attractive option for commuters. In addition, AI can help identify areas where additional public transportation services are needed, helping to improve access to transportation in underserved communities. The Tokyo Metropolitan Government's AI-powered transportation system, which utilizes an algorithm to determine the most efficient route for buses to take based on real-time traffic data. The system analyzes the data to provide passengers with real-time information on bus arrival times and the expected journey time to their destination. This has improved the overall experience of commuters and reduced the time spent waiting for buses.

Finally, AI can be used to improve the overall efficiency of public transportation systems. By optimizing routes and schedules, AI can help reduce the number of vehicles needed to provide public transportation services. This can help reduce the cost of operating public transportation systems and make them more financially sustainable in the long term. In addition, AI can help identify areas where improvements are needed, such as the installation of new bus stops or the construction of new train stations.

AI-powered transportation systems are also gaining popularity in the United States. For instance, in Los Angeles, the GoLA app uses AI algorithms to provide real-time updates on public transportation options, including buses and trains. The app utilizes real-time traffic data to help commuters avoid congestion and plan their journeys efficiently. This has made it easier for commuters to navigate the complex Los Angeles public transportation system and reduce wait times for public transportation options.

Another example of an AI-powered transportation system is the NextBus system in San Francisco. The NextBus system uses real-time data on bus locations to provide accurate arrival times to passengers, improving the overall reliability of the bus system and encouraging more people to use public transportation.

It is no doubt that traffic congestion is a major issue in many cities, leading to lost productivity, increased pollution, and frustrated citizens. However, by leveraging emerging technologies like AI, we can improve traffic flow, reduce congestion, and enhance public transportation. AI-powered traffic management systems, smart traffic lights, predictive analytics, and enhanced public transportation systems are just a few examples of how technology can be used to address this critical issue. With continued investment in these technologies, we can create more efficient and sustainable transportation systems that benefit both citizens and the environment.

Chapter 3: Enhancing Citizen Services with AI Chatbots

AI-powered chatbots are becoming increasingly popular in many industries, and local government is no exception. These intelligent chatbots have transformed the way citizens interact with government services, from getting information about programs to processing applications for government services. In this chapter, we will explore how chatbots can be used to improve citizen services and provide examples of successful chatbot implementations in local government.

Chatbots are AI-powered digital assistants that can simulate human conversation. They can answer common questions, provide information about programs and services, and even process applications. Chatbots use natural language processing (NLP) algorithms to understand user requests and respond appropriately. They are available 24/7, which means citizens can get the information they need at any time without having to wait for business hours.

One of the biggest benefits of chatbots is their ability to increase efficiency and reduce costs. Chatbots can handle a large volume of requests and inquiries simultaneously without requiring additional staff. They can also process applications quickly and accurately, reducing errors and improving processing times. As a result, chatbots can help local governments save time and money while improving citizen services.

There are many successful chatbot implementations in local government. For example, the City of Las Vegas has implemented a chatbot named "Ask L.V." that has helped the city reduce call volumes and wait times while improving citizen satisfaction. Ask L.V. answers common questions about city services, events, and regulations, providing citizens with quick and easy access to information. The chatbot uses natural language processing to understand citizen questions and provide helpful answers. By reducing the number of calls and inquiries that the city receives, Ask L.V. has helped to reduce the workload of city staff, allowing them to focus on more complex issues.

The City of Los Angeles has implemented a chatbot named "Chip" to process parking ticket appeals. Chip has helped the city reduce processing times from six weeks to less than one week while reducing appeals processing costs. Chip uses artificial intelligence to analyze citizen appeals and provide a decision in a matter of minutes. This has greatly improved citizen satisfaction with the appeals process and has reduced the workload of city staff.

But it's not just Las Vegas and Los Angeles that are implementing chatbots in local government. Many other cities across the United States are also using chatbots to improve citizen services. For example, Citibot is an AI-powered chatbot that is used by several local governments to improve citizen engagement. Citibot allows citizens to report issues and receive updates on the status of their requests, improving transparency and accountability in local government.

One of the most significant benefits of using chatbots in local governments is increased efficiency, as they can handle citizen inquiries around the clock. By providing quick and accurate answers to citizen questions, chatbots can significantly reduce the workload of city staff, enabling them to focus on more complex tasks.

The COVID-19 pandemic has only highlighted the importance of chatbots in local government. With the increased number of calls classified as "difficult" due to pandemic-related problems, chatbots can ease the burden on city staff and provide an effective solution to citizen inquiries. Chatbots can also provide citizens with information about regulations, laws, and policies, as well as critical personal information and processes, which may otherwise be difficult to obtain.

Another significant advantage of using chatbots in local government is the cost-effectiveness. Employing chatbots is 30% cheaper than hiring a live agent, which can result in significant cost savings for the city. Chatbots can also provide consistent answers to citizen inquiries, which avoids confusion and minimizes the spread of misinformation.

Citizens also benefit from chatbots as they can receive quick and accurate answers to their questions around the clock. This improves citizen satisfaction, reduces wait times, and enhances overall customer experience. Chatbots can also provide citizens with links to relevant city services and resources, enabling them to access critical information at their convenience.

Chatbots are not limited to just answering citizen inquiries; they can also be used to automate internal communication and processes within the city. For instance, chatbots can be used in the onboarding process, where new employees can ask the chatbot questions and receive immediate answers, reducing the need to contact various departments.

In today's fast-paced world, businesses and local governments need to ensure that they're providing high-quality customer service while keeping costs low. Chatbots offer a solution to this dilemma by providing a cost-effective alternative to traditional customer service methods. One of the significant benefits of chatbots is their ability to handle a large volume of inquiries at a low cost. By automating customer service, chatbots can reduce the workload of city staff and allow them to focus on more complex tasks.

Chatbots are a one-time investment, with costs ranging from $1,000 to $5,000 per month for development and maintenance. Compared to hiring additional staff, using chatbots is significantly cheaper, with a study by Chatbot Magazine indicating that companies can benefit from a 30% cost reduction on customer service after implementing a chatbot system. Furthermore, research predicts that chatbots will save businesses $8 billion by 2022. This cost reduction potential makes chatbots an attractive option for local governments looking to redirect resources towards more pressing issues.

By using chatbots, local governments can provide 24/7 support to citizens without the need for additional staff. Chatbots can handle a wide range of inquiries, including simple questions about city services, events, and regulations, which make up most inquiries. This allows staff to focus on more complex inquiries and critical tasks while reducing the workload and stress on employees. In addition, chatbots provide consistent answers to frequently asked questions, which minimizes confusion among citizens and reduces the spread of misinformation.

Chatbots are revolutionizing the way local governments interact with their citizens. They not only provide information on government programs, answer frequently asked questions, and process applications for government services but also provide personalized recommendations and gather feedback from citizens. This technology has the potential to transform citizen services in local government, by increasing efficiency, reducing costs, and improving citizen satisfaction.

For instance, the city of San Francisco has implemented a chatbot named "MySF" that provides personalized recommendations for services and programs based on a citizen's location and interests. MySF has improved citizen engagement and participation in city programs and events. Similarly, the city of Boston uses a chatbot named "CityBot" to gather feedback from citizens on city services and programs, which has helped the city identify areas for improvement and make changes to better serve its citizens.

Chatbots are available 24/7, which means citizens can access the relevant information or ask their questions anytime. They can handle a large volume of inquiries at a low cost, reducing the need for additional staff. Furthermore, chatbots can provide consistent and accurate responses, and if they do not have the answer, they can transfer users to an agent or direct them to a self-service knowledge center. Chatbots can also be programmed to analyze text for keyword combinations and generate a relevant response, which allows for more flexible and natural conversations.

Chatbots can help local governments better understand and meet the needs of their citizens by providing personalized recommendations and gathering feedback. As chatbot technology continues to improve, we can expect to see more successful chatbot implementations in local government. Successful implementations in cities like Las Vegas, Los Angeles, San Francisco, and Boston demonstrate that chatbots have the potential to significantly improve citizen services in local government.

Chapter 4: Streamlining Procurement Processes with AI

Procurement processes in local government are known to be complex and time-consuming. From identifying potential vendors to the bid evaluation process, procurement activities require significant human efforts and resources. However, with the advent of artificial intelligence (AI), it is now possible to streamline these processes and achieve better outcomes in terms of efficiency, cost savings, and transparency. In this book, we will explore the benefits of AI-powered procurement processes and how they can be implemented in local governments.

The procurement process in local government involves a series of activities that start with identifying a need for goods or services and end with contract management. This process can be complex and time-consuming, requiring significant human resources and involving multiple stakeholders, including procurement officers, department heads, and vendors.

Procurement planning is the first stage of the procurement process that involves identifying the need for goods or services and developing a plan to acquire them. This stage includes developing specifications, identifying potential suppliers, and determining the procurement method that will be used. To effectively plan procurement, it is important to consider several factors. The first factor is the type of procurement needed. There are four main types of procurement: direct procurement, indirect procurement, services procurement, and construction procurement. Direct procurement is the obtainment of goods, materials, or services that a business can use to generate profit through the production of an end-product or resale. Indirect procurement involves the purchase of goods or services that are not directly used in the production of goods or services, such as office supplies or maintenance services. Services procurement involves the purchase of services, such as consulting or legal services. Construction procurement is the obtainment of services and goods needed for the construction of a facility.

The second factor to consider when planning procurement is the need for the goods or services. This involves identifying the specifications of the goods or services needed, including the quality, quantity, and delivery requirements. Once the need has been identified, potential suppliers can be identified. This involves researching potential suppliers, obtaining quotes and proposals, and evaluating the suppliers based on their ability to meet the specifications and requirements. The procurement method that will be used should also be determined in this stage. There are several procurement methods, including competitive bidding, sole source procurement, and request for proposal (RFP).

To effectively plan procurement, it is important to have a clear understanding of the organization's goals and objectives. This involves collaborating with stakeholders, including department heads and procurement officers, to ensure that the procurement plan aligns with the organization's overall strategy. It is also important to consider the budget and funding available for procurement activities. This can involve developing a procurement budget and identifying potential funding sources.

The second stage of the procurement process is source selection, which involves identifying potential vendors and soliciting bids or proposals. In this stage, procurement officers need to evaluate various vendors based on criteria such as price, quality, and past performance. The choice of vendors is critical as it affects the quality of goods or services procured and the overall cost of the procurement process. Therefore, procurement officers must use a systematic approach to vendor selection, which may involve evaluating proposals and bids based on various factors and subfactors specified in the solicitation documents.

Vendor evaluation may involve several methods, such as the lowest price technically acceptable (LPTA) process or best value tradeoff (BVT) process. In the LPTA process, the vendor with the lowest price that meets the specified technical requirements is selected, while in the BVT process, the vendor is selected based on a tradeoff between price and other factors such as quality and past performance.

Procurement officers must ensure that the evaluation process is fair and transparent, and that proposals or bids are evaluated based on the factors and subfactors specified in the solicitation documents. The evaluation process may involve a team of experts who have the knowledge and expertise to evaluate vendors based on various criteria. After the evaluation, procurement officers may issue a purchase order (PO) to the selected vendor.

The bid evaluation process is an important stage in the procurement process that involves reviewing and evaluating bids or proposals received from potential vendors. According to one source, the bid evaluation process can be classified into four basic stages: (1) preliminary examination for responsiveness to formal qualification requirements, (2) evaluation for compliance with technical requirements, (3) price/financial evaluation, and (4) post qualification/due diligence.

To properly evaluate bids, it is important to choose the right evaluation team for your procurement. Small groups work better than just one person, bringing a balanced perspective to the scoring process. During the financial evaluation stage, eligible offers are compared with the financial, commercial, and resource requirements specified in the solicitation document. The financial evaluation must be conducted only on technically qualified bids.

Contrary to popular belief, the lowest bid does not always win. The most popular way to pick the best vendor or service provider is the MEAT criteria, which stands for "most economically advantageous tender." Apart from the cost, other criteria such as quality, past performance, and delivery times are considered when evaluating bids. A standardized approach and set expectations can ensure that there is no subjectivity when making a judgment on the proposals made.

The bid evaluation process is a critical aspect of strategic sourcing and directly correlates with the overall performance of the procurement process. The supplier evaluation and appraisal criteria determine a significant portion of the procurement process's performance. Regular vendor performance evaluations provide an opportunity to establish benchmarks and goals from beginning to end, which is crucial for vendor performance management and strategic sourcing.

To evaluate bids, a thorough analysis is required to determine which vendor offers the best value for money. The evaluation should be on an item-by-item basis, and full technical compliance with stated appendices achieves the maximum score. Bid responses with minor acceptable deviations are also considered. A grading system is used to evaluate bid sections based on evaluation criteria, bid strategies, additions, and deletions.

The fourth stage in the procurement process is quality assurance, which involves verifying that the goods or services meet the required specifications and quality standards. This stage is critical in ensuring that the procured goods or services meet the necessary quality standards to meet the expectations of the buyers and end-users. The process of quality assurance involves a series of activities aimed at verifying that the goods or services meet the required quality standards.

One of the main activities in the quality assurance process is careful monitoring and inspection of the goods or services. This involves comparing the delivered goods or services with the specified requirements and quality standards. Any deviations or non-conformance to the required quality standards are identified and reported to the supplier for corrective action.

Another important activity in the quality assurance process is testing the goods or services. This testing process involves a thorough evaluation of the goods or services to ensure that they meet the required specifications and quality standards. The testing process may include functional testing, performance testing, load testing, security testing, and other types of tests as required by the specific goods or services.

Quality assurance also involves ongoing evaluation of the supplier's performance to ensure that they consistently deliver goods or services that meet the required quality standards. The quality assurance team may use performance metrics and key performance indicators (KPIs) to measure the supplier's performance and identify areas for improvement. This ongoing evaluation helps to maintain a high level of quality and continuous improvement of the goods or services.

Contract management is a crucial process that involves various stages to ensure that contracts are effectively managed from start to finish. The final stage of contract management is focused on the ongoing management of the contract and ensuring that all obligations and commitments are met. This stage is critical in ensuring that the contract is fulfilled in accordance with the agreed terms and conditions.

Contract management involves monitoring vendor performance, handling disputes and claims, and ensuring that all contractual obligations are met. This includes ensuring that the vendor meets its obligations and that payments are made on time. The contract manager is responsible for overseeing the day-to-day operations of the contract and ensuring that all activities are carried out in accordance with the contract.

In addition to monitoring performance, the contract management stage also involves managing any disputes or claims that may arise during the contract term. This may include negotiating solutions or taking legal action if necessary. It is important to maintain good communication with the vendor and document any changes or modifications made to the contract.

The procurement process is a critical aspect of any organization's operations. It involves the systematic process of sourcing and purchasing goods and services necessary for the organization's functions. The procurement process is usually long and arduous, with many people lost and confused. The process involves several steps, such as identifying the need for goods and services, creating a purchase request, identifying, and selecting a supplier, negotiating terms, and pricing, and issuing a purchase order.

One common frustration with the procurement process is the time it takes to deliver services, especially for high-tech items. In some cases, the procurement process can take so long that new versions of products are released before the procurement process finishes. This can lead to a significant delay in obtaining the latest and most up-to-date products, which can put organizations at a disadvantage.

In many cases, constituents are frustrated by the time it takes to deliver services because they do not understand the laws that control the purchasing process. Procurement policies and procedures are typically complex, and it can be challenging to understand the rules and regulations that govern the procurement process. To address this issue, organizations can develop purchasing policies that create a policy structure aligned with the organization's strategic purchasing requirements.

Overall, the procurement process requires significant attention and effort from all stakeholders involved. Organizations should develop a robust procurement process that ensures the timely delivery of goods and services while complying with all applicable laws and regulations. To do so, organizations can employ due diligence practices, such as conducting background checks and reviewing financial statements, to identify and select reliable suppliers. By developing effective procurement policies and procedures, organizations can streamline the procurement process and ensure that their constituents are satisfied with the services delivered.

The procurement process in local government can be streamlined and made more efficient using artificial intelligence (AI).AI can be used to automate certain tasks, such as identifying potential vendors and evaluating bids, which can save time and reduce costs.

However, the good news is that the use of artificial intelligence (AI) can significantly improve its efficiency. AI can automate various tasks such as identifying potential vendors, evaluating bids, and analyzing contracts to ensure compliance with regulations This can save time and reduce costs associated with manual procurement processes.

AI-powered tools can also help with data analytics, allowing governments to analyze large amounts of data and gain insights into supplier performance and market trends. By identifying patterns and trends, governments can better forecast demand and optimize their procurement strategies, leading to more efficient and cost-effective procurement processes.

Furthermore, AI can assist in ensuring fairness and transparency in the procurement process. By automating tasks, AI can reduce the potential for human error and bias in supplier selection and evaluation. This can help prevent any accusations of favoritism or corruption and maintain public trust in the procurement process.

The benefits of AI-powered procurement in local government include increased efficiency, reduced costs, and improved transparency. AI can help to eliminate bias in the procurement process, ensuring that all vendors are given a fair chance to compete for contracts.

Artificial intelligence (AI) has the potential to transform the procurement process in local government by increasing efficiency, reducing costs, and improving transparency. By automating certain tasks, such as identifying potential vendors and evaluating bids, AI can save time and reduce costs. AI can also help procurement professionals to make more informed decisions by providing additional insights based on complex sets of data.

One of the major benefits of AI-powered procurement is the elimination of bias in the procurement process, which ensures that all vendors are given a fair chance to compete for contracts. With the use of AI, procurement officers can also identify possible ethical conflicts or problems with a supplier before they become serious issues.

Moreover, AI-powered procurement can provide decision-makers with the ability to identify inefficiencies and potential cost savings in the products and services they purchase.

To maximize the benefits of AI in procurement, organizations need to define the public benefit of using AI and assess risks, incorporate relevant legislation and codes of practice, and articulate the feasibility of accessing relevant data. Furthermore, automation of the procurement cycle should be done in steps, starting with mapping the current procurement process.

AI-powered procurement in local government can significantly improve efficiency, reduce costs, and increase transparency. By eliminating bias, identifying potential ethical conflicts, and providing valuable insights to decision-makers, AI can help procurement officers make more informed decisions and ensure that all vendors are given a fair chance to compete for contracts. However, it is important for organizations to follow relevant legislation and codes of practice and assess risks associated with using AI.

Chapter 5: Improving Public Health with AI (Stop)

Artificial Intelligence (AI) has become an essential tool for improving public health in numerous ways. One of the primary ways AI can be used is through the development of AI-powered healthcare systems, which include telemedicine and personalized healthcare.

In recent years, advancements in telecommunication technologies have brought about a significant shift in healthcare delivery. Telemedicine, also known as telehealth, is the delivery of healthcare services remotely using telecommunication technologies. It has opened a new world of possibilities for patients who have limited access to healthcare services due to geographical, financial, or other reasons. With the help of AI-powered telemedicine systems, remote diagnosis and treatment of patients has become possible, leading to improved patient outcomes and reduced healthcare costs.

One of the major benefits of telemedicine is its ability to provide healthcare services to patients who live in rural or remote areas, where access to healthcare services is limited. In such areas, patients may have to travel long distances to reach a healthcare facility, which can be costly and time-consuming. Moreover, the limited availability of healthcare providers in these areas may result in delayed diagnosis and treatment, leading to poor health outcomes. Telemedicine can bridge this gap by allowing patients to access healthcare services from the comfort of their own homes.

AI-powered telemedicine systems can improve the accuracy and efficiency of remote diagnosis and treatment. These systems can use machine learning algorithms to analyze patient data and provide healthcare providers with real-time insights. For example, an AI-powered telemedicine system can analyze a patient's symptoms and medical history to provide a diagnosis and suggest a treatment plan.

This can help healthcare providers make informed decisions and reduce the risk of misdiagnosis.

Advancements in technology have opened new doors in healthcare and personalized medicine, allowing for customized treatments and preventative measures for individuals. AI-powered systems have proven to be an effective tool in providing personalized healthcare, which can help reduce the risk of chronic diseases and improve overall health outcomes.

One of the major advantages of AI-powered personalized healthcare is the ability to analyze large amounts of data, including an individual's genetic information, health history, and lifestyle factors. By analyzing this data, AI systems can identify patterns and make recommendations that are tailored to the individual's specific needs. This can include personalized treatment plans, preventative measures, and lifestyle changes that can improve their overall health and wellbeing.

In addition to providing personalized treatment plans, AI-powered systems can also help healthcare providers monitor patients remotely. Remote patient monitoring can be especially beneficial for individuals with chronic conditions, such as diabetes, heart disease, and asthma. By using wearable devices and other connected health technologies, healthcare providers can monitor patients' vital signs and receive alerts if any abnormalities are detected. This allows for early intervention and can prevent serious health complications from occurring.

Another advantage of AI-powered personalized healthcare is the potential to improve clinical trial design and drug development. By using AI to analyze large amounts of patient data, researchers can identify subpopulations that are more likely to respond to certain treatments or therapies. This can help reduce the time and cost associated with clinical trials and drug development, and ultimately lead to more effective treatments for patients.

However, there are also potential drawbacks to AI-powered personalized healthcare. One concern is the risk of data breaches and privacy violations. Healthcare providers and researchers must take measures to ensure that patient data is securely stored and protected. Additionally, there is the potential for AI systems to perpetuate existing biases and inequalities in healthcare. It is important to ensure that AI-powered healthcare systems are developed and implemented in an ethical and equitable manner.

Despite these concerns, the potential benefits of AI-powered personalized healthcare are significant. By providing customized treatment plans and preventative measures, healthcare providers can help reduce the risk of chronic diseases and improve overall health outcomes for individuals. Remote patient monitoring and improved clinical trial design can also lead to more efficient and effective healthcare delivery. As technology continues to advance, AI-powered personalized healthcare will likely play an increasingly important role in public health.

AI has the potential to revolutionize the way we analyze healthcare data and inform public health policy. With the vast amount of data available, it is crucial to use advanced technologies to extract meaningful insights and make informed decisions. AI-powered systems can help in this regard, by processing and analyzing large datasets to identify trends and patterns that can be used to inform public health policy.

One of the most important applications of AI in public health is disease surveillance. AI algorithms can analyze vast amounts of healthcare data, including electronic health records, insurance claims, and public health data, to identify risk factors for disease outbreaks, track the spread of infectious diseases, and predict future outbreaks. For instance, the Google Flu Trends project uses search query data to estimate flu activity in different regions of the world. By tracking changes in search behavior, the system can provide early warning of flu outbreaks and help public health officials take proactive measures to prevent the spread of the disease.

In addition to disease surveillance, AI can also be used to identify gaps in healthcare services and develop targeted interventions to improve public health outcomes. For example, by analyzing healthcare data, AI algorithms can identify populations that are at higher risk of developing certain diseases and provide personalized recommendations for preventative measures. This can help reduce the risk of chronic diseases and improve overall health outcomes.

One notable example of the use of AI in public health is the Precision Medicine Initiative launched by the US National Institutes of Health (NIH). This initiative aims to use genetic and health data to develop personalized treatment plans for patients based on their individual characteristics. AI algorithms can analyze genetic data to identify genetic mutations that may be associated with certain diseases and develop targeted therapies to treat those conditions. Similarly, AI algorithms can analyze health data to identify risk factors for certain diseases and provide personalized recommendations for preventative measures.

Another example of the use of AI in public health is the development of predictive models for disease outbreaks. For instance, researchers at the University of California, San Francisco, have developed an AI system that can predict the spread of the Zika virus by analyzing data on human travel patterns and mosquito populations. The system uses machine learning algorithms to identify patterns and trends in the data and predict the likelihood of an outbreak in different regions of the world. By providing early warning of potential outbreaks, the system can help public health officials take proactive measures to prevent the spread of the disease.

Advancements in artificial intelligence (AI) are transforming the healthcare industry and are increasingly being used to inform public health policy. One area where AI can be particularly valuable is in analyzing healthcare utilization data to identify patterns and trends that can inform resource allocation and healthcare spending decisions.

By analyzing large datasets, AI algorithms can identify areas where healthcare utilization is high and where targeted interventions may be most effective in reducing costs and improving health outcomes. For example, AI-powered analytics can identify high-utilization patient populations and potential causes, such as lack of access to primary care or chronic conditions that may require more proactive management. This information can inform the development of targeted interventions, such as expanding access to primary care or implementing chronic care management programs.

Moreover, AI can also help in predicting future healthcare utilization patterns, which can inform resource allocation decisions. Machine learning algorithms can analyze past utilization patterns and identify trends that may indicate future demand for healthcare services. For example, if data analysis shows an increase in the number of patients seeking treatment for a particular condition, policymakers can allocate resources to prevent a potential surge in demand.

Additionally, AI can be used to identify disparities in healthcare utilization and inform policies to address them. For example, by analyzing healthcare utilization data by race or income, AI can identify disparities in access to care and inform policies to improve access for under-served populations. This can be particularly important in the context of the COVID-19 pandemic, which has highlighted existing disparities in healthcare utilization and outcomes.

One example of AI being used to inform resource allocation decisions is the work being done by the Veterans Health Administration (VA) in the United States. The VA has implemented an AI-powered analytics platform to identify high-risk patients who are likely to require intensive care unit (ICU) admission. By identifying these patients early, the VA has been able to allocate resources more efficiently and provide early interventions to improve outcomes.

Similarly, AI is being used in the United Kingdom's National Health Service to predict demand for hospital services, enabling policymakers to allocate resources more effectively and improve patient outcomes.

While AI has the potential to revolutionize healthcare utilization analysis and inform public health policy, there are also challenges to be addressed. One of the biggest challenges is ensuring that the data used to inform AI algorithms is accurate and representative. Bias in the data can lead to biased algorithms, which can perpetuate disparities in healthcare utilization and outcomes. Additionally, concerns around privacy and data security must be addressed to ensure that sensitive healthcare data is protected.

In conclusion, AI has the potential to transform the analysis of healthcare utilization data and inform public health policy decisions. By identifying patterns and trends in healthcare utilization, policymakers can make informed decisions about resource allocation and healthcare spending, improving health outcomes and reducing costs. While there are challenges to be addressed, the potential benefits of AI in healthcare utilization analysis are significant and warrant further exploration and investment.

Chapter 6: Enhancing Emergency Management with AI

Emergency management is an essential function of local government. In recent years, advancements in artificial intelligence (AI) have shown great potential to improve emergency response efforts. AI-powered emergency response systems can help local governments to identify potential emergencies, respond to them quickly, and minimize the impact on the community. In this chapter, we will discuss the various ways AI can be used to enhance emergency response efforts, including early warning systems for natural disasters, predictive analytics for emergency planning, and the use of AI-powered robots for search and rescue operations in hazardous environments.

Early Warning Systems for Natural Disasters

Natural disasters such as earthquakes, tsunamis, hurricanes, and floods can cause devastating consequences, including loss of life, displacement, and damage to infrastructure. Early warning systems can help minimize the impact of these disasters by providing advanced warning to local communities and governments. AI-powered early warning systems have the potential to improve the accuracy and speed of alerts, enabling rapid and effective response to natural disasters.

The early earthquake warning system developed by the Japan Meteorological Agency (JMA) is an excellent example of how AI can be used to develop an effective early warning system for natural disasters. The system uses AI algorithms to analyze seismic data collected from more than 1,000 sensors across Japan in real-time. When an earthquake occurs, the system quickly analyzes the seismic waves to estimate the location, magnitude, and intensity of the earthquake. The system then issues an alert to local governments and the public within seconds of detection.

The alerts provided by the early earthquake warning system are critical for people living in earthquake-prone areas. These alerts provide vital information on the location and magnitude of the earthquake, as well as the estimated arrival time of the seismic waves. This information enables people to take immediate action to protect themselves and their property. For example, people can move to a safe location, secure their belongings, and shut off gas and water supplies to prevent further damage.

In addition to issuing alerts, the JMA's early earthquake warning system can also help emergency responders prepare for earthquakes. By providing information on the location, magnitude, and intensity of the earthquake, emergency responders can better allocate resources and respond more effectively to the disaster. This can help to minimize the impact of the earthquake and reduce the number of casualties.

The success of the JMA's early earthquake warning system has inspired other countries to develop similar systems. For example, the United States Geological Survey (USGS) has developed an early warning system for earthquakes called ShakeAlert. ShakeAlert uses similar AI algorithms to analyze seismic data and issue alerts to local governments and the public. The system has been tested in California and is currently being rolled out across the west coast of the United States.

The AI-based early warning system developed by the Indian Space Research Organisation (ISRO) is a powerful tool to predict floods in India. The country is prone to floods, and they cause significant damage to life and property every year. The system developed by ISRO uses satellite imagery to identify potential flood-prone areas and monitor water levels in real-time. The data is collected from various sources, including satellite images, weather data, and ground sensors. The system uses machine learning algorithms to analyze the data and identify potential flood risk areas.

The system has been successfully deployed in several regions of India, including the states of Assam, Bihar, and Kerala, which are known to be flood-prone regions. The system provides early warnings of floods, which allows the local governments to take measures to protect their citizens and minimize the damage caused by floods. The alerts include information on the severity of the flood, the potential areas affected, and the likely time of arrival of the floodwaters. This information is critical in helping the local governments to make informed decisions and take proactive measures to protect their citizens.

The system has several benefits over traditional flood prediction methods. Firstly, it provides real-time data, which allows for more accurate predictions of potential floods. The system can monitor water levels in real-time, which provides an accurate assessment of the potential flood risk in a particular area. Secondly, the system is cost-effective and easy to deploy. It uses existing satellite and sensor infrastructure, which means that the cost of deployment is relatively low. Thirdly, the system can be easily scaled up to cover large areas. This is particularly important in a country like India, where floods can occur in multiple regions simultaneously.

In addition to early warning systems for floods and earthquakes, AI can also be used for early warning systems for other natural disasters such as hurricanes, tornadoes, and tsunamis. For example, the National Oceanic and Atmospheric Administration (NOAA) in the United States has developed an AI-powered system to predict hurricanes. The system uses machine learning algorithms to analyze weather data and predict the path and intensity of hurricanes. This information is critical in helping local governments and communities to prepare for the potential impact of hurricanes and take measures to protect their citizens.

Overall, AI-powered early warning systems have the potential to significantly improve the accuracy and speed of natural disaster alerts, enabling communities to take proactive measures to protect themselves and their property.

Predictive Analytics for Emergency Planning

Predictive analytics is an important tool that local governments can use to anticipate and prepare for emergencies. By analyzing historical data, predictive analytics can help local governments identify potential emergency situations before they occur, allowing them to take proactive measures to mitigate the impact of the disaster.

One example of the use of predictive analytics is in identifying areas that are prone to natural disasters. By analyzing historical data on floods, hurricanes, and other natural disasters, local governments can identify areas that are at high risk of these events. They can then take proactive measures to mitigate the impact of these disasters. For example, they may build sea walls to protect against flooding, or relocate residents in high-risk areas to safer locations.

In addition to identifying areas prone to natural disasters, predictive analytics can also be used to identify other potential emergency situations. For example, by analyzing data on crime rates and accidents, local governments can identify areas that are at high risk of these events. They can then take measures to increase police presence or improve road safety in these areas to reduce the likelihood of emergencies.

Predictive analytics can also be used to improve emergency response efforts when disasters do occur. By analyzing data on previous emergency situations, local governments can identify patterns and trends in how emergencies unfold. They can then use this information to improve emergency response efforts, such as by improving communication systems or deploying emergency personnel more effectively.

One example of the use of predictive analytics in emergency response is in the field of firefighting. Fire departments can use predictive analytics to identify areas that are at high risk of wildfires, allowing them to allocate resources more effectively. For example, they may station firefighters in high-risk areas during periods of high fire danger or conduct controlled burns to reduce the risk of wildfires.

There have been several other examples of fire departments using predictive analytics to identify areas at high risk for fires in recent years. One such example is the Los Angeles Fire Department (LAFD), which has implemented a predictive analytics system called FireStat LA. This system uses historical data on fires and other risk factors to identify areas that are at high risk for fires and allocate resources accordingly.

Similarly, the San Francisco Fire Department has developed a predictive analytics tool called the Fire Department Intelligence Tool (FIT), which analyzes data on factors such as building age, fire history, and vegetation to identify areas that are at high risk for fires. The system then provides recommendations for targeted outreach and preventative measures, such as brush clearance or building retrofits, to reduce the risk of fires in those areas.

In addition to city fire departments, some rural fire departments have also started to implement predictive analytics systems. For example, the Ashland Fire Department in Oregon has developed a predictive analytics model that uses data on weather, fuel loads, and other risk factors to identify areas that are at high risk for wildfires. The model then provides recommendations for preventative measures, such as creating fire breaks or increasing the number of firefighters in high-risk areas.

Another example of the use of predictive analytics in emergency response is in the field of public health. Public health officials can use predictive analytics to identify areas that are at high risk of disease outbreaks, allowing them to allocate resources more effectively. For example, they may deploy mobile clinics to areas with high rates of infectious diseases or launch public health campaigns to encourage vaccination or hand washing in high-risk areas.

In addition to identifying potential emergency situations and improving emergency response efforts, predictive analytics can also be used to evaluate the effectiveness of emergency response strategies. By analyzing data on emergency response efforts, local governments can identify which strategies are most effective and which may need to be improved. For example, they may analyze response times to identify areas where response efforts can be improved or track the outcomes of emergency interventions to determine which interventions are most effective in mitigating the impact of disasters.

Some examples show how predictive analytics can be used to evaluate the effectiveness of emergency response strategies, identify areas for improvement, and target resources more effectively. By using data-driven insights, local governments and emergency services can improve their ability to prevent emergencies and respond to disasters when they do occur:

1. Los Angeles Fire Department (LAFD): The LAFD is using predictive analytics to evaluate the effectiveness of its emergency response efforts. The department is using data on response times, call volumes, and other factors to identify areas where response efforts can be improved. This includes identifying which fire stations are busiest and which areas are most prone to fires, allowing the department to allocate resources more effectively.

2. New York City Fire Department (FDNY): The FDNY is using predictive analytics to evaluate the effectiveness of its fire prevention efforts. The department is analyzing data on fire incidents and building inspections to identify which buildings are most at risk of fires. This information is used to target fire prevention efforts, including building inspections and outreach to residents.

3. Chicago Fire Department: The Chicago Fire Department is

using predictive analytics to evaluate the effectiveness of its emergency medical services (EMS). The department is analyzing data on EMS response times, patient outcomes, and other factors to identify areas where response efforts can be improved. This includes identifying which neighborhoods have the highest incidence of cardiac arrests and which EMS interventions are most effective in improving patient outcomes.

4. Australian Fire and Emergency Services: The Australian Fire and Emergency Services (AFES) is using predictive analytics to identify areas at high risk of bushfires. The AFES is using data on weather patterns, vegetation growth, and other factors to identify areas where bushfires are most likely to occur. This information is used to target fire prevention efforts, including fuel reduction programs and community education campaigns.

5. London Fire Brigade: The London Fire Brigade is using predictive analytics to evaluate the effectiveness of its fire safety inspections. The brigade is analyzing data on building characteristics, inspection results, and fire incidents to identify which buildings are most at risk of fires. This information is used to target fire safety inspections and outreach to building owners and residents.

Overall, predictive analytics is a valuable tool for local governments in identifying potential emergencies, planning for their occurrence, and improving emergency response efforts. By using historical data to identify patterns and trends, local governments can take proactive measures to reduce the risk of emergencies and improve emergency response efforts when disasters do occur.

AI-Powered Robots for Search and Rescue

Operations

Natural disasters, such as earthquakes, hurricanes, and wildfires, can cause extensive damage to infrastructure and homes, displace communities, and result in loss of life. During such events, search and rescue operations can be challenging, and emergency responders often face hazardous and life-threatening conditions. However, with the advancements in technology, AI-powered robots have become an increasingly valuable tool in disaster response and recovery efforts.

This chapter will discuss the use of AI-powered robots in search and rescue operations and the benefits they offer. We will also explore the different types of robots used in disaster response and recovery efforts, including drones and ground-based robots.

Drones in Disaster Response and Recovery

Drones have become an increasingly important tool in disaster response and recovery efforts, particularly in search and rescue operations. Equipped with advanced sensors and AI algorithms, drones can be flown over inaccessible or hazardous areas to identify individuals who may need assistance. In addition, they can be used to identify areas that need immediate attention, such as damaged infrastructure or areas prone to flooding.

One of the most notable examples of the use of drones in disaster response occurred during Hurricane Harvey in 2017. The massive hurricane caused widespread devastation in Texas and Louisiana, resulting in over 100 fatalities and billions of dollars in damages. In response to the disaster, the Federal Aviation Administration (FAA) issued special authorizations to allow drones to fly in the affected areas to assist in search and rescue operations. These drones were equipped with cameras and AI algorithms that allowed them to identify individuals who were stranded or in need of assistance. The use of drones in this disaster response effort allowed for a more efficient and effective search and rescue operation, ultimately saving lives, and reducing the impact of the disaster on affected communities.

In addition to natural disasters, drones equipped with AI algorithms can also be used in response to man-made disasters, such as building collapses or industrial accidents. For example, in 2021, a building in Surfside, Florida collapsed, resulting in the deaths of nearly 100 people. Drones equipped with AI algorithms were used in the search and rescue efforts, providing aerial footage of the collapsed building, and identifying areas where survivors may be located. The use of drones in this disaster response effort allowed for a more efficient and targeted search and rescue operation, improving the chances of locating survivors and reducing the impact of the disaster on affected communities.

Drones equipped with AI algorithms can also be used in disaster response and recovery efforts to assess damage and identify areas that need immediate attention. For example, after Hurricane Maria devastated Puerto Rico in 2017, drones were used to assess the damage to critical infrastructure, such as bridges and power lines, and identify areas where immediate repairs were necessary. The use of drones in this disaster response effort allowed for a more efficient and effective recovery operation, improving the speed and accuracy of repairs, and reducing the impact of the disaster on affected communities.

Another example of the use of drones in disaster response occurred during the California wildfires in 2020. Drones equipped with AI algorithms were used to map the extent of the wildfires and identify areas that needed immediate attention. The use of drones in this disaster response effort allowed for a more efficient and effective firefighting operation, improving the speed and accuracy of containment efforts, and reducing the impact of the wildfires on affected communities.

In addition to search and rescue operations and damage assessment, drones equipped with AI algorithms can also be used in disaster response and recovery efforts for environmental monitoring. For example, after the Deepwater Horizon oil spill in 2010, drones were used to monitor the extent of the spill and identify areas where cleanup efforts were necessary. The use of drones in this disaster response effort allowed for a more efficient and effective cleanup operation, improving the speed and accuracy of containment, and reducing the impact of the spill on affected ecosystems.

Other more recent examples of the use of drones are:

1. In January 2022, drones were used to assist with disaster response efforts in Tonga following the eruption of an underwater volcano. The drones were used to survey the affected areas and assess the damage caused by the eruption.

2. In February 2022, drones were used to assist with disaster response efforts in India following a cyclone. The drones were used to survey the affected areas and identify areas in need of immediate attention, such as damaged infrastructure and areas prone to flooding.

3. In March 2022, drones were used to assist with disaster response efforts in Greece following a severe storm. The drones were used to survey the affected areas and identify areas in need of immediate attention, such as damaged infrastructure and areas prone to flooding.

4. In April 2022, drones were used to assist with disaster response efforts in Mexico following a volcanic eruption. The drones were used to survey the affected areas and assess the damage caused by the eruption.

5. In May 2022, drones were used to assist with disaster response efforts in Hawaii following a volcanic eruption. The drones were used to survey the affected areas and assess the damage caused by the eruption.

Chapter 6: Ground-Based Robots in Disaster Response and Recovery

Ground-based robots equipped with AI algorithms have the potential to play a vital role in disaster response and recovery efforts. These robots can be used to perform hazardous tasks, such as search and rescue operations and debris removal, which may pose a significant risk to human responders.

One example of the use of ground-based robots in disaster response is during the Fukushima nuclear disaster in Japan in 2011. The radiation levels in the affected areas were too high for human responders to enter safely. As a result, robots were used to assist in debris removal and other tasks in the affected areas. These robots were equipped with sensors and other technologies that allowed them to navigate through complex environments and identify potential hazards.

In 2023 and into the future, we can expect to see more advancements in ground-based robots equipped with AI algorithms, with an increased focus on disaster response and recovery efforts. For instance, the use of robots equipped with advanced sensors and cameras can help first responders assess the damage caused by natural disasters like earthquakes or hurricanes. They can also be used to identify survivors and deliver aid to those in need.

Another example is the use of drones equipped with AI algorithms to assist in disaster response efforts. These drones can be used to survey disaster-stricken areas and identify areas in need of aid quickly and efficiently. They can also be used to deliver medical supplies, food, and other essentials to people in isolated or hard-to-reach areas. In 2019, drones equipped with AI algorithms were used to assist in the response to Hurricane Dorian in the Bahamas.

Finally, robots equipped with AI algorithms can also be used in search and rescue operations. For example, in 2018, a team of researchers from Texas A&M University developed a robotic snake that can be used in search and rescue operations. The robot is equipped with sensors that allow it to detect human breath and locate people trapped in debris. The robot can also navigate through narrow spaces an

Ground-based robots equipped with artificial intelligence algorithms can be an invaluable tool in the face of both natural and industrial disasters. In addition to being used to assess damage caused by natural disasters such as earthquakes or hurricanes and identify survivors in need of aid, they can also be used in industrial disasters such as oil spills and chemical explosions. For example, robots equipped with specialized sensors can be deployed to detect toxic chemicals and other hazardous materials, allowing for safer and more effective cleanup efforts.

One of the major advantages of using ground-based robots in disaster response and recovery efforts is the increased safety they provide to humans involved in the cleanup process. In industrial disasters, for example, robots can be used to explore and map out areas affected by toxic chemicals or hazardous materials. This can help to minimize human exposure to dangerous substances, reducing the risk of injury or death. Furthermore, robots can be equipped with advanced sensors and cameras that enable them to identify hazards and assess damage in real-time. This information can be used to make more informed decisions about the best course of action for cleanup efforts.

One example of the use of ground-based robots in disaster response and recovery efforts is the Wall-Ye robot, which is designed to autonomously prune grapevines in the wine industry. Although this robot was not designed specifically for disaster response, it illustrates the potential for robots to take over dangerous or tedious tasks in industries where human workers are at risk of injury. Similarly, in the case of industrial disasters, robots equipped with specialized sensors and other tools can be used to perform tasks that would otherwise be too dangerous or difficult for human workers.

Another area where ground-based robots can be used in disaster response and recovery efforts is in the search for survivors. A swarm of autonomous flying robots has been implemented in simulation to cooperatively gather situational awareness data during the first few hours after a major natural disaster. In computer simulations, the swarm is successful in locating over 90% of survivors in less than an hour. While this technology is still in the early stages of development, it has the potential to significantly improve the speed and effectiveness of search and rescue efforts in the aftermath of natural disasters.

The use of ground-based robots equipped with AI algorithms and specialized sensors is not without its challenges, however. One major obstacle to the widespread adoption of these technologies is their high cost. Robots capable of performing complex tasks such as detecting hazardous materials can be prohibitively expensive, making it difficult for smaller companies and organizations to invest in these technologies. Another challenge is the need for specialized training and expertise to operate and maintain these robots, which can be a significant barrier for many organizations.

The use of ground-based robots equipped with AI algorithms and specialized sensors has the potential to revolutionize disaster response and recovery efforts in both natural and industrial disasters. These robots can provide valuable insights into the extent of damage caused by disasters, identify survivors in need of aid, and perform dangerous or tedious tasks that would otherwise put human workers at risk. However, significant challenges remain, including the high cost and need for specialized training to operate these technologies. Despite these challenges, the potential benefits of ground-based robots in disaster response and recovery efforts make them an exciting area of development for researchers and companies alike.

Benefits of AI-powered Robots in Disaster Response and Recovery

The use of AI-powered robots in disaster response and recovery efforts has the potential to provide significant benefits. These robots can be used to assist in search and rescue operations in hazardous environments, reducing the risk of injury or death for human responders. In addition, they can be used to identify areas that need immediate attention, allowing for a more efficient and effective response effort.

One of the main benefits of using AI-powered robots in disaster response is their ability to operate in hazardous environments. In situations where the risk of injury or death is high, robots can be used to search for survivors, collect data, and provide real-time information to first responders. This allows human responders to focus on tasks that require human decision-making, while robots take on the more dangerous and repetitive tasks.

Another benefit of using AI-powered robots in disaster response is their ability to quickly and accurately identify areas that need immediate attention. Using sensors and other data collection tools, robots can gather information about the disaster area and provide real-time data to response teams. This information can be used to prioritize response efforts, allowing for a more efficient and effective response effort.

In addition to search and rescue operations, AI-powered robots can also be used to assist in debris removal and other hazardous tasks. For example, robots can be used to detect and remove hazardous materials, reducing the risk of exposure to human responders. This allows for a more thorough and efficient response effort, as robots can operate in areas that may be too hazardous for human responders.

One example of the use of AI-powered robots in disaster response is the use of drones for search and rescue operations. Drones equipped with cameras and other sensors can be used to search for survivors and collect data in areas that may be too dangerous for human responders. In addition, drones can be used to assess damage and identify areas that need immediate attention. This allows for a more efficient and effective response effort, as response teams can focus their efforts on areas that require immediate attention.

Another example of the use of AI-powered robots in disaster response is the use of autonomous ground vehicles for debris removal. These vehicles can be equipped with sensors and other tools to detect and remove hazardous materials, reducing the risk of exposure to human responders. In addition, these vehicles can operate in areas that may be too hazardous for human responders, allowing for a more thorough and efficient response effort.

The use of AI-powered robots in disaster response and recovery efforts also has the potential to improve coordination between response teams. By providing real-time data and information, robots can help response teams work more efficiently and effectively, reducing the risk of duplication of efforts or missed opportunities.

However, it is important to note that the use of AI-powered robots in disaster response and recovery efforts is not without challenges. One challenge is the need for specialized training and expertise to operate and maintain these robots. In addition, there may be concerns about the cost and availability of these technologies, particularly in low-resource settings.

Despite these challenges, the potential benefits of using AI-powered robots in disaster response and recovery efforts are significant. These technologies have the potential to improve the efficiency and effectiveness of response efforts, while reducing the risk of injury or death for human responders. As such, it is likely that we will continue to see increased use of AI-powered robots in disaster response and recovery efforts in the coming years.

Limitations of AI-powered Robots in Disaster

Response and

The use of AI-powered robots in disaster response and recovery efforts can offer numerous benefits, including reducing the risk of injury or death for human responders, identifying areas in need of immediate attention, assisting in debris removal and hazardous tasks, and assessing hazardous environments. However, there are also limitations to their use, including the cost of the robots and their maintenance and the limitations of the robots' ability to navigate complex environments.

According to, AI-powered robots can reduce the risk of injury or death for human responders by assisting in search and rescue operations in hazardous environments. Additionally, they can identify areas that need immediate attention, allowing for a more efficient and effective response effort. These robots can also be used to assist in debris removal and other hazardous tasks, reducing the risk of injury or exposure to hazardous materials for human responders.

However, one of the main limitations of the use of AI-powered robots in disaster response and recovery efforts is the cost of the robots and their maintenance. As noted by, understanding, and addressing the limitations of AI-powered robots is required to realize their benefits. The cost of purchasing and maintaining these robots may limit their use in some disaster response and recovery efforts.

Another limitation is the ability of AI-powered robots to navigate through complex environments, such as collapsed buildings or flooded areas. According to, some robots may have difficulty navigating through these environments, which may limit their effectiveness in some search and rescue operations. However, continued development in robotics and AI technology may address these limitations over time.

Despite these limitations, the potential benefits of AI-powered robots in emergency management are significant. For example, they can be used to assess hazardous environments, as noted by. Robots can be equipped with sensors and technologies, allowing them to navigate through hazardous environments and identify potential hazards, while also increasing the speed and accuracy of disaster response efforts. Additionally, AI-powered robots have potential applications in other areas of emergency management, such as fire suppression and hazardous material handling.

However, the use of AI-powered robots in emergency management also raises ethical and safety concerns. For example, there is a risk that the use of robots may reduce the importance of human expertise in disaster response and recovery efforts, as noted by. Additionally, there are concerns about the safety of robots and their impact on the environment. It is important for local governments to carefully consider the potential benefits and risks of using AI-powered robots in emergency management, and to implement appropriate safety measures and ethical guidelines.

AI can be used to enhance emergency response efforts in various ways. AI-powered early warning systems can improve the accuracy and speed of alerts, allowing local governments to respond quickly to potential disasters. Predictive analytics can be used to identify potential emergencies and plan, accordingly, reducing the risk of emergencies and improving emergency response efforts. AI-powered robots can be used to assist with search and rescue operations and other hazardous tasks, improving the safety of emergency responders. As AI technology continues to advance, it is likely that it will play an increasingly important role in emergency management and response efforts.

Chapter 7: Optimizing Waste Management with AI

Waste management is a major challenge for local governments, and AI can be used to optimize waste management processes. In this chapter, we will explore the use of AI-powered waste management systems, including smart trash cans and predictive analytics for waste collection.

Waste management is an essential aspect of modern life, and as our societies continue to grow and consume, it becomes more critical than ever to manage waste effectively. Traditional waste management methods are often inefficient, costly, and can have significant negative impacts on the environment. However, recent advances in artificial intelligence (AI) technology are now providing new opportunities for optimizing waste management processes and reducing the overall impact of waste on our environment.

In this chapter, we will explore the use of AI-powered waste management systems, including smart trash cans and predictive analytics for waste collection. We will also discuss the benefits and challenges of using AI in waste management, as well as the ethical considerations and potential future developments in this field

Introduction to AI-powered waste management systems

AI-powered waste management systems are a relatively new development that aim to revolutionize the way we manage waste. These systems leverage machine learning and predictive analytics to optimize the collection, transportation, and disposal of waste. They are based on a network of sensors, cameras, and other data collection devices that are installed in trash cans, waste sorting facilities, and other locations where waste is generated or processed.

The primary objective of AI-powered waste management systems is to collect data on waste generation, composition, and disposal patterns. This data is then analyzed to develop predictive models that can anticipate future waste generation patterns and help local governments to plan for the most efficient and cost-effective waste management strategies. The use of AI-powered waste management systems can help reduce costs, increase efficiency, and improve the overall effectiveness of waste management programs.

One of the key benefits of AI-powered waste management systems is their ability to accurately sort different types of waste. This is accomplished using AI-powered robots, which can work long hours at a consistent speed, and with an AI-powered waste-detection capability that is as accurate as the human eye. For recycling facilities, this means enhanced outputs, increased productivity, and reduced costs.

AI-powered waste management systems can also help reduce the environmental impact of waste by identifying recyclable materials and diverting them away from landfills. This is accomplished using AI-powered sensors, which can identify the composition of waste and sort it accordingly. This not only reduces the amount of waste that ends up in landfills but also helps to conserve natural resources by promoting the reuse and recycling of materials.

Another benefit of AI-powered waste management systems is their ability to optimize waste collection routes. This is accomplished using predictive analytics, which can anticipate future waste generation patterns and help local governments to plan the most efficient collection routes. By reducing the amount of time and resources required for waste collection, local governments can reduce costs and improve the overall efficiency of their waste management programs.

AI-powered waste management systems can also help improve public health and safety. By identifying hazardous materials and diverting them away from landfills, these systems can help reduce the risk of pollution and other environmental hazards. Additionally, by optimizing waste collection routes and reducing the amount of time that waste spends in transit, these systems can help reduce the risk of disease transmission and other public health risks associated with waste management.

There are several challenges associated with the adoption of AI-powered waste management systems. One of the biggest challenges is the high cost of implementing these systems. This includes the cost of installing sensors, cameras, and other data collection devices, as well as the cost of developing and maintaining the predictive analytics models that drive these systems. Additionally, there may be regulatory and legal barriers to the adoption of these systems, particularly in areas where waste management is heavily regulated

AI-Based Waste Monitoring

Waste management is one of the most pressing issues facing our planet today. With the global population on the rise, and our cities becoming increasingly urbanized, the amount of waste we generate is only going to increase. To manage this waste effectively, we need to find new and innovative ways to optimize waste management processes, reduce waste generation, and improve the efficiency of waste disposal. One of the most promising technologies for achieving these goals is artificial intelligence (AI).

One of the primary applications of AI in waste management is waste monitoring. Waste monitoring involves the use of sensors and cameras to monitor waste generation, collection, and disposal. These sensors and cameras can be placed in a variety of locations, including waste bins, collection trucks, and waste disposal sites. Once installed, they can collect data on the amount of waste generated, the frequency of waste collection, and the efficiency of waste disposal.

AI algorithms can then be used to analyze this data and identify trends and patterns. These algorithms can be trained to recognize different types of waste, such as plastics, paper, and organic waste, and to track the movement of this waste through the waste management system. By analyzing this data, waste management companies can identify areas of inefficiency in their operations and take steps to optimize these processes.

For example, AI algorithms can be used to identify areas where waste is being generated at a higher rate than usual. This information can be used to adjust waste collection schedules, ensuring that waste is collected more frequently in these areas. Similarly, AI can be used to identify areas where waste is being generated at a lower rate than usual. This information can be used to adjust waste collection schedules, reducing the frequency of waste collection in these areas, and saving resources.

AI can also be used to optimize the routing of waste collection vehicles. By analyzing data on the location of waste bins and the frequency of waste collection, AI algorithms can identify the most efficient routes for waste collection vehicles to take. This can help to reduce the time and resources needed to collect waste, while also reducing emissions from these vehicles.

Another application of AI in waste management is the identification of waste contamination. When waste is contaminated with materials that cannot be recycled or composted, it can reduce the effectiveness of waste management processes and increase the amount of waste that ends up in landfills. By using AI to analyze data on the composition of waste, waste management companies can identify contaminated waste and take steps to remove it from the waste stream.

One example of this is the use of AI to identify food waste in waste streams. By analyzing data on the composition of waste, AI algorithms can identify the presence of food waste and alert waste management companies to its presence. Waste management companies can then take steps to divert this waste to composting facilities, where it can be turned into fertilizer for use in agriculture.

AI can also be used to improve the efficiency of waste disposal. By analyzing data on the composition of waste, AI algorithms can identify materials that can be recycled or composted, and those that must be disposed of in landfills. This information can be used to optimize waste disposal processes, ensuring that materials are disposed of in the most environmentally friendly way possible.

For example, AI can be used to identify materials that can be recycled, such as plastics, paper, and metals. Waste management companies can then take steps to separate these materials from the waste stream and send them to recycling facilities. Similarly, AI can be used to identify materials that can be composted, such as organic waste. Waste management companies can then take steps to divert this waste to composting facilities, where it can be turned into fertilizer for use in agriculture.

AI-Based Waste Sorting

Waste sorting is an important aspect of waste management, as it allows for the separation of recyclable materials from non-recyclable waste. This separation is crucial for reducing the amount of waste that ends up in landfills and increasing the amount of waste that is recycled. AI can play a significant role in improving waste sorting processes, making them more efficient and effective.

One example of AI-enabled waste sorting is the use of robotics. Robots can be programmed to sort waste based on various criteria, such as size, shape, and material type. For example, ZenRobotics, a Finnish company, has developed robotic arms that can sort construction and demolition waste, identifying and separating materials such as metal, wood, and concrete. Similarly, AMP Robotics, a Colorado-based company, has developed a robotic system that can sort mixed waste streams, using computer vision and machine learning to identify different types of materials.

AI can also be used in waste sorting using imaging technologies, such as hyperspectral imaging and X-ray fluorescence. Hyperspectral imaging can be used to identify the chemical composition of different materials, while X-ray fluorescence can be used to identify the elemental composition of materials. These technologies can be integrated into waste sorting systems to improve the accuracy of material identification, allowing for more efficient and effective sorting.

One example of AI-enabled waste sorting using imaging technologies is the TOMRA Sorting Solutions system, which uses X-ray transmission and hyperspectral imaging to sort plastic waste. The system can identify and separate different types of plastics, such as PET, HDPE, and PVC, improving the efficiency of plastic recycling processes.

Another example of AI-enabled waste sorting is the use of machine learning algorithms to identify different types of waste. Machine learning algorithms can be trained on large datasets of waste images to recognize different types of materials, allowing for more accurate and efficient waste sorting. For example, the company Wasteless has developed a waste sorting system that uses machine learning to identify and sort different types of waste, such as paper, cardboard, plastics, and metals.

Overall, AI-enabled waste sorting can significantly improve the efficiency and effectiveness of waste management processes. By using robotics, imaging technologies, and machine learning algorithms, waste can be sorted more accurately and efficiently, reducing the amount of waste that ends up in landfills and increasing the amount of waste that is recycled.

AI-Based Predictive Maintenance

Waste management equipment, such as garbage trucks and recycling facilities, are essential for the effective management of waste. However, like all equipment, they are subject to wear and tear, and breakdowns can cause significant disruptions to waste management operations. To prevent these disruptions, waste management companies have traditionally relied on scheduled maintenance routines that are based on the manufacturer's recommendations or a predetermined schedule.

However, these approaches to maintenance are not always effective, as they may not consider the unique operating conditions of a particular piece of equipment or the actual wear and tear that it experiences. As a result, equipment failures can still occur, resulting in costly downtime and lost productivity.

To address this issue, many waste management companies are turning to predictive maintenance, a strategy that uses AI algorithms to predict when equipment is likely to fail and to schedule maintenance before it occurs. Predictive maintenance is a form of condition-based maintenance that relies on real-time data from sensors, cameras, and other sources to monitor the health and performance of equipment.

By analyzing this data, AI algorithms can identify patterns and trends that indicate when a piece of equipment is likely to fail. For example, sensors may detect vibrations or changes in temperature that indicate that a motor is about to fail. By detecting these changes early, maintenance teams can schedule repairs before the motor fails, preventing costly downtime and reducing the risk of more serious damage.

Another advantage of predictive maintenance is that it allows waste management companies to optimize their maintenance schedules. By scheduling maintenance when it is most needed, companies can avoid unnecessary downtime and reduce the frequency of maintenance, which can save time and money.

One example of a company that has successfully implemented predictive maintenance in waste management is Veolia. Veolia is a French multinational company that provides waste management services to municipalities and businesses around the world. In 2018, the company announced that it was using predictive maintenance to optimize the performance of its garbage trucks.

Veolia installed sensors on its garbage trucks that measure the temperature of the oil in the engine and the vibration of the engine components. This data is sent to an AI algorithm that analyzes it to identify patterns that indicate when a component is likely to fail. When the algorithm detects a potential problem, it alerts maintenance teams, who can schedule repairs before the truck breaks down.

By implementing predictive maintenance, Veolia was able to reduce the downtime of its garbage trucks by up to 50%. This allowed the company to provide more efficient waste management services to its customers and to reduce its maintenance costs.

In addition to predictive maintenance, AI can also be used to optimize the operation of waste management equipment. For example, AI algorithms can be used to optimize the routes that garbage trucks take when collecting waste. By analyzing data on traffic patterns, road conditions, and the location of waste containers, AI algorithms can identify the most efficient routes for garbage trucks to take. This can reduce fuel consumption, lower emissions, and improve the efficiency of waste collection.

One example of a company that has used AI to optimize waste collection routes is the city of Barcelona. In 2018, the city introduced an AI-powered waste management system that uses data from sensors on garbage trucks to optimize waste collection routes. The system analyzes data on traffic patterns, the location of waste containers, and the amount of waste in each container to identify the most efficient route for each garbage truck.

The system has been highly effective, reducing the distance that garbage trucks travel by up to 12%. This has reduced the amount of fuel that is used for waste collection and has lowered emissions from garbage trucks.

AI can also be used to optimize the operation of recycling facilities. For example, AI algorithms can be used to analyze data on the types and amounts of waste that are being processed at a recycling facility. By analyzing this data, the algorithms can identify opportunities to increase the efficiency of the recycling process

AI-Based Route Optimization

Waste management is an important aspect of modern society, and with the increasing population, it is becoming more and more challenging to manage waste efficiently. To tackle this challenge, artificial intelligence (AI) has emerged as a powerful tool for waste management. AI can be used to optimize various aspects of waste management, including waste monitoring, waste sorting, equipment optimization, and route optimization.

Route optimization is a crucial component of waste management. Waste collection is a complex process that involves the collection of waste from different areas, transportation to the treatment facility, and finally, disposal. It is essential to optimize waste collection routes to reduce the time and resources required for waste collection, which can help to reduce costs and improve the efficiency of waste management processes.

Traditionally, waste collection routes were optimized based on manual methods, such as using a map and compass. However, this method is inefficient and prone to errors. It is also difficult to account for factors such as traffic congestion and changes in waste generation patterns. With the emergence of AI, it is now possible to optimize waste collection routes more efficiently and effectively.

AI algorithms can analyze data related to waste collection routes, including waste generation patterns, the location of waste collection points, and traffic patterns. This data can be used to optimize waste collection routes, reducing the time and resources required for waste collection. By optimizing waste collection routes, it is possible to reduce the number of collection vehicles required, which can reduce costs and improve the efficiency of waste management processes.

One example of the use of AI for route optimization in waste management is the Smart Waste Collection System (SWCS) developed by the University of Sheffield. The SWCS uses AI algorithms to optimize waste collection routes based on data related to waste generation patterns, the location of waste collection points, and traffic patterns. The SWCS has been tested in the city of Sheffield in the UK and has been shown to reduce the number of collection vehicles required by up to 20%. This has led to a reduction in carbon emissions, as well as a reduction in costs for waste management companies.

Another example of the use of AI for route optimization in waste management is the Waste Wizard developed by Rubicon Global. The Waste Wizard uses AI algorithms to analyze data related to waste generation patterns, the location of waste collection points, and traffic patterns. This data is used to optimize waste collection routes, reducing the time and resources required for waste collection. The Waste Wizard has been implemented in several cities in the US, including Philadelphia and Atlanta, and has been shown to reduce the number of collection vehicles required by up to 50%.

The benefits of using AI for route optimization in waste management are numerous. By optimizing waste collection routes, it is possible to reduce the time and resources required for waste collection, which can help to reduce costs and improve the efficiency of waste management processes. Additionally, by reducing the number of collection vehicles required, it is possible to reduce carbon emissions, which can help to reduce the environmental impact of waste management.

However, there are also some challenges associated with the use of AI for route optimization in waste management. One of the main challenges is the quality of the data used to optimize waste collection routes. It is essential to ensure that the data used is accurate and up to date, as any errors or inconsistencies can lead to suboptimal route optimization. Additionally, there may be resistance to change from waste management companies that are used to traditional methods of waste collection route optimization.

Route optimization is an important application of AI in waste management. AI algorithms can be used to optimize waste collection routes, reducing the time and resources required for waste collection. This can help to reduce costs and improve the efficiency of waste management processes. There are some challenges associated with the use of AI for route optimization, such as ensuring the quality of

Challenges and Limitations

While the potential benefits of using AI in waste management are clear, it is important to recognize the challenges and limitations that come with this technology. One of the primary challenges is the availability of data. For AI algorithms to be effective, they require large amounts of data to analyze. However, waste management data is often limited and fragmented, making it difficult for AI systems to be trained and optimized.

For example, in developing countries, waste management data may be scarce or nonexistent. Without accurate data, it is difficult to develop effective waste management strategies or to train AI systems to optimize waste management processes. Additionally, in some regions, waste management data may be collected by multiple agencies, resulting in inconsistent or incomplete data sets. This fragmentation makes it difficult to develop a comprehensive view of waste management practices and to identify areas where improvements can be made.

Another challenge related to the use of AI in waste management is the issue of ethics and privacy. As AI systems collect and analyze data related to waste management practices, there is a risk that personal or sensitive information may be inadvertently shared. For example, an AI system may collect data on the types of waste generated by a particular household or business, potentially revealing sensitive information about the habits or practices of the people who live or work there.

To address these challenges, it is important to take a proactive approach to data management and privacy. This can include developing clear data sharing and privacy policies, as well as investing in secure data storage and analysis systems. It is also important to work collaboratively with waste management agencies and stakeholders to ensure that data is collected consistently and accurately across all sectors.

Furthermore, to address the challenge of limited data availability, waste management agencies can work to develop partnerships with private companies and academic institutions to expand data collection and analysis efforts. For example, AI startups may be able to provide specialized expertise in developing AI algorithms for waste management, while universities and research institutes can provide valuable data and analysis on waste generation and disposal.

Despite these challenges, the potential benefits of using AI in waste management are too significant to ignore. AI algorithms can help to optimize waste management processes, reduce waste generation, and increase the efficiency of waste disposal. By addressing the challenges of data availability and privacy, waste management agencies can unlock the full potential of AI in this important field.

One example of successful implementation of AI in waste management comes from the city of Barcelona. In 2018, the city launched a pilot project in which AI algorithms were used to optimize waste collection routes. The system analyzed data on waste generation, collection routes, and vehicle locations to identify the most efficient routes for collecting waste. The project resulted in a 20% reduction in vehicle emissions and a 30% reduction in waste collection costs.

Another example comes from the city of Amsterdam, which has developed a waste sorting system that uses AI to identify and separate different types of waste. The system analyzes data from sensors and cameras to identify recyclables and non-recyclables, reducing the amount of waste that ends up in landfills and increasing the amount that is recycled.

While there are challenges and limitations to using AI in waste management, the potential benefits are too significant to ignore. By addressing the challenges of data availability and privacy, and working collaboratively with private companies and academic institutions, waste management agencies can unlock the full potential of AI in this important field. With AI, we can optimize waste management processes, reduce waste generation, and increase the efficiency of waste disposal, leading to a cleaner and more sustainable future.

AI has shown great promise in the field of waste management, with its ability to optimize processes, reduce waste, and increase recycling rates. However, there are also challenges and limitations that must be addressed to fully realize the potential of AI in this area.

One of the main challenges is the availability of data. AI algorithms require large amounts of data to be effective, and waste management data is often limited. For example, in some developing countries, waste management data may not be systematically collected or available in digital format, making it difficult to apply AI algorithms effectively. To overcome this challenge, governments and waste management organizations should prioritize data collection and management, ensuring that data is collected in a consistent and standardized manner and made available in a digital format.

Another challenge is the development of effective AI algorithms. AI algorithms must be able to accurately identify and classify different types of waste and predict trends in waste generation and disposal. This requires a deep understanding of the waste management process and the factors that influence waste generation and disposal. Researchers and waste management organizations should collaborate to develop more effective AI algorithms that can address the unique challenges of waste management.

In addition to technical challenges, there are also ethical and privacy concerns related to the use of AI in waste management. For example, there are concerns about the use of AI to monitor individuals' waste disposal habits, which could be seen as an invasion of privacy. To address these concerns, it is important to establish clear guidelines and regulations regarding the use of AI in waste management, with a focus on protecting individual privacy and ensuring transparency in the use of AI algorithms.

Despite these challenges, AI has already shown significant promise in waste management. For example, AI algorithms have been used to optimize waste collection routes, reducing the amount of time and resources required for waste collection and improving the efficiency of the waste management process. Similarly, AI algorithms have been used to predict equipment failures and schedule maintenance, reducing downtime, and improving the overall performance of waste management equipment.

AI can also be used to sort waste more effectively, reducing the amount of waste that ends up in landfills and increasing the amount of waste that is recycled. For example, AI algorithms can be used to identify different types of waste and sort them based on their recyclability. This can help reduce the amount of contamination in recycling streams and increase the overall efficiency of the recycling process.

Chapter 8: Improving Public Housing with AI

Public housing is a critical part of urban housing policy, providing affordable and safe housing to low-income households. However, providing adequate public housing is a significant challenge in most cities worldwide. Despite significant investments in public housing over the years, the quality of housing and the living conditions in public housing often do not meet expectations.

One of the main challenges in public housing is maintenance and repair. Public housing often suffers from poor maintenance and neglect, leading to deteriorating living conditions and lower quality of life for residents. AI can be leveraged to improve maintenance and repair in public housing. For example, predictive maintenance algorithms can be used to identify potential maintenance issues before they occur, allowing housing authorities to schedule repairs before they become major problems. Additionally, AI can be used to optimize repair schedules, reducing the time and resources required for maintenance and improving the efficiency of public housing management.

Another important application of AI in public housing is energy management. Energy costs can be a significant burden for low-income households and reducing energy costs can improve the affordability of public housing. AI algorithms can be used to optimize energy usage in public housing, reducing energy waste and lowering energy costs. For example, smart thermostats can be installed in public housing units, allowing residents to control their heating and cooling while also enabling AI algorithms to optimize energy usage based on occupancy patterns and weather conditions.

AI can also be used to improve safety and security in public housing. Crime and vandalism are major concerns in public housing, and security measures are often limited. AI algorithms can be used to analyze security footage and identify potential security threats. For example, facial recognition algorithms can be used to identify potential intruders, and machine learning algorithms can be used to predict patterns of criminal activity and allocate security resources accordingly. Additionally, AI can be used to improve fire safety in public housing, using predictive analytics to identify potential fire hazards and improve fire response times.

One of the most significant challenges in public housing is providing adequate social services to residents. Low-income households often face significant social and economic challenges, such as unemployment, homelessness, and mental health issues. AI can be used to improve social services in public housing, providing residents with access to the resources they need to thrive. For example, AI algorithms can be used to analyze data related to resident needs and identify potential areas for intervention. Additionally, AI can be used to improve communication between residents and housing authorities, allowing residents to voice their concerns, and providing housing authorities with valuable feedback on the quality of housing and services.

While AI has significant potential in the field of public housing, there are also challenges and limitations that must be addressed. One of the main challenges is the ethical and privacy concerns related to the use of AI in public housing. AI algorithms often rely on large amounts of personal data, raising concerns about data privacy and security. Additionally, there are concerns about the potential for AI algorithms to reinforce existing biases and inequalities in public housing.

To address these concerns, it is essential to develop transparent and accountable AI systems that are designed to address the specific needs of public housing residents. This includes developing AI systems that are designed to minimize bias and promote fairness, as well as establishing clear guidelines for data privacy and security. Additionally, it is important to involve public housing residents in the development and implementation of AI systems, ensuring that their needs and concerns are considered throughout the process.

Overview of Public Housing

Public housing has been a cornerstone of housing policy in many countries for decades, with the aim of providing safe, affordable housing to low-income families who may not be able to afford housing in the private market. However, despite significant investments in public housing over the years, the quality of housing and living conditions for many residents of public housing has often fallen short of expectations. This is where the potential of artificial intelligence (AI) comes in, as it can help to improve the quality and efficiency of public housing operations, as well as enhance the living conditions of residents.

One area where AI can have a significant impact on public housing is in maintenance and repairs. As public housing properties age, they require increasingly frequent repairs and maintenance to remain habitable. However, traditional methods of maintenance can be slow, inefficient, and costly. With AI, it is possible to create a more efficient maintenance system by using sensors and other IoT devices to monitor the condition of buildings and predict maintenance needs. This allows for proactive maintenance, reducing the need for costly emergency repairs and improving the overall quality of housing.

For example, in Singapore, the Housing & Development Board (HDB) has implemented an AI-powered predictive maintenance system in its public housing estates. The system uses sensors to monitor the condition of building elements such as lifts, water pumps, and air conditioning systems. The data collected by these sensors is then analyzed by an AI algorithm to predict when maintenance is required, allowing for proactive maintenance, and reducing the likelihood of equipment breakdowns. This has resulted in a reduction in maintenance costs, improved equipment performance, and higher levels of resident satisfaction.

Another area where AI can improve public housing is in energy efficiency. Public housing properties can consume large amounts of energy, resulting in high costs for both residents and housing authorities. With AI, it is possible to optimize energy use and reduce costs by analyzing data on energy consumption patterns and identifying opportunities for energy savings. For example, the city of New York is using AI to optimize the heating and cooling systems in public housing buildings, resulting in significant energy savings and reduced costs for residents.

AI can also help to improve the overall living conditions of public housing residents. For example, AI-powered smart home systems can be used to monitor indoor air quality, detect potential hazards such as water leaks or gas leaks, and adjust heating and cooling systems to optimize comfort levels. Smart home systems can also provide residents with greater control over their living environment, allowing them to adjust lighting, temperature, and other settings to their individual preferences.

In addition, AI can be used to improve the allocation of public housing resources. By analyzing data on occupancy rates, demographics, and other factors, it is possible to allocate public housing resources more efficiently and effectively. This can help to ensure that resources are distributed in a way that maximizes their impact and benefits the most people possible.

However, there are also challenges associated with the use of AI in public housing. One of the main challenges is the cost of implementing AI systems, which can be prohibitive for some housing authorities. In addition, there are concerns around data privacy and security, as well as the potential for AI systems to perpetuate bias and discrimination. These issues must be addressed to ensure that AI is used in a responsible and ethical manner.

AI has the potential to significantly improve the quality and efficiency of public housing operations, as well as enhance the living conditions of residents. From proactive maintenance to energy efficiency to smart home systems, AI can help to create a more sustainable and livable public housing environment. However, it is important to address the challenges and limitations associated with the use of AI in public housing, to ensure that it is used in a responsible and ethical manner that benefits everyone.

The Role of AI in Public Housing

AI has the potential to transform public housing by enabling better management of buildings, reducing maintenance costs, and improving the living conditions of residents. By harnessing the power of AI, public housing authorities can optimize resource allocation, improve operational efficiency, and enhance the overall quality of housing. Here are some examples of how AI can be applied in the context of public housing

Building Health and Safety Monitoring

AI has the potential to revolutionize the way public housing is managed and maintained, with the ability to detect and respond to building health and safety issues being one of its most promising applications. One of the main benefits of using AI in this context is the ability to monitor buildings in real-time, allowing for quick and effective responses to potential issues.

For example, AI-powered sensors can be used to detect mold and water damage in buildings. These sensors can be placed in various areas of the building, such as the walls, floors, and ceilings, to detect any signs of moisture. If an issue is detected, AI algorithms can analyze the data to determine the extent of the problem and recommend the appropriate course of action. This could include repairs, improvements to ventilation systems, or other measures to prevent further damage.

In addition to detecting moisture and mold, AI can also be used to monitor air quality in public housing. Poor air quality is a common issue in public housing, often due to a lack of proper ventilation systems or the presence of environmental pollutants such as asbestos or lead. AI-powered sensors can detect changes in air quality and alert building managers to potential issues. This can enable quick responses to air quality issues, such as the installation of air filters or the identification and removal of pollutants.

AI can also be used to detect potential safety hazards in public housing buildings. For example, sensors can be used to monitor the structural integrity of buildings, detecting potential issues such as cracks in walls or foundation problems. This data can then be analyzed by AI algorithms to determine the severity of the problem and recommend appropriate action, such as repairs or reinforcement. Additionally, AI can be used to monitor for potential fire hazards, such as overheating electrical systems, and alert building managers to potential risks.

By using AI to monitor the health and safety of public housing buildings, building managers can be more proactive in addressing issues before they become more severe. This can help to reduce the overall cost of maintenance and repairs, while also improving the quality of life for residents. Additionally, AI can help public housing authorities to better allocate resources, ensuring that funds are directed towards the areas of greatest need.

Another way in which AI can be used to transform public housing is through the automation of maintenance tasks. Public housing buildings require a significant amount of maintenance, from regular cleaning to repairs and upgrades. By automating some of these tasks using AI, public housing authorities can reduce the overall cost of maintenance and improve the efficiency of the maintenance process.

For example, AI-powered robots can be used to clean common areas of public housing buildings, such as hallways and stairwells. These robots can be programmed to operate during off-peak hours, reducing disruptions to residents. Additionally, AI algorithms can be used to detect maintenance issues, such as malfunctioning appliances or broken fixtures, and automatically schedule repairs or replacements.

By automating maintenance tasks, public housing authorities can ensure that buildings are properly maintained while also freeing up resources for other areas of need. This can help to reduce the overall cost of maintenance and improve the overall quality of life for residents.

AI can also be used to optimize energy use in public housing buildings. Energy costs can be a significant burden for low-income households and reducing energy use can help to make public housing more affordable. By using AI to monitor energy use in public housing buildings, building managers can identify areas where energy use can be reduced and implement strategies to reduce consumption.

For example, AI algorithms can analyze data on energy use to identify patterns and trends. This data can be used to identify areas where energy use is particularly high, such as during peak hours or in certain areas of the building. By implementing strategies to reduce energy use in these areas, such as installing energy-efficient appliances or improving insulation, building managers can help to reduce energy costs for residents.

By using AI to monitor and optimize energy use, public housing authorities can significantly reduce their energy costs and carbon footprint. AI algorithms can analyze data from smart meters and other sensors to identify patterns in energy use and recommend ways to reduce energy consumption. For example, AI can suggest the best times for residents to use energy-intensive appliances such as washing machines and dishwashers or recommend upgrades to energy-efficient lighting and HVAC systems.

AI can also be used to optimize the allocation of resources in public housing, ensuring that resources are directed to where they are most needed. For example, AI-powered predictive models can be used to forecast maintenance needs and prioritize repairs based on factors such as the severity of the issue, the impact on residents, and the availability of resources. This can help public housing authorities make better use of their limited resources, reducing costs and improving the overall quality of public housing.

Another important application of AI in public housing is in community engagement. By leveraging AI-powered chatbots and other communication tools, public housing authorities can improve communication with residents and provide better support services. Chatbots can be used to answer common questions, provide information on available services and resources, and even offer personalized support to residents in need. This can help to build stronger, more resilient communities and improve the quality of life for residents.

AI can also be used to help public housing authorities better understand the needs of their residents and develop more effective policies and programs. By analyzing data on resident demographics, health, and social status, AI-powered predictive models can identify factors that contribute to poor health outcomes and social inequality. This can help public housing authorities to develop targeted interventions that address the root causes of these issues, such as providing access to health services or education programs.

However, the use of AI in public housing is not without its challenges and limitations. One of the main challenges is the need to ensure that AI algorithms are fair and unbiased. Public housing authorities must be careful to avoid using AI in ways that perpetuate social inequality or discrimination. For example, AI-powered predictive models must be trained on diverse data sets to avoid bias and ensure that interventions are targeted at those who need them most.

Another challenge is the need to protect the privacy and security of residents. Public housing authorities must be transparent about how they collect and use data and must ensure that residents have control over their personal data. This requires strong data governance policies and practices, as well as effective cybersecurity measures to protect against data breaches and other security threats.

AI has the potential to transform public housing by enabling better management of buildings, reducing maintenance costs, improving living conditions for residents, and promoting community engagement. However, to fully realize this potential, public housing authorities must address the challenges and limitations associated with the use of AI, including ensuring fairness and privacy. With continued innovation and investment, AI can help to build more equitable and sustainable communities for all.

Automated Maintenance

AI has the potential to revolutionize the maintenance and management of public housing by automating routine tasks and enabling predictive maintenance. By using AI-powered sensors, public housing authorities can monitor the condition of buildings in real-time, detect maintenance issues as they arise, and even automate responses to prevent further damage. This approach can help public housing authorities identify and address issues more quickly and efficiently, reducing costs and improving the living conditions of residents.

One example of this approach in action is the use of AI-powered sensors to detect water leaks in public housing buildings. Water leaks can cause significant damage to buildings and can be expensive to repair. By using sensors to detect leaks in real-time, public housing authorities can quickly identify and address the problem before it escalates, reducing the amount of damage and the associated costs. This approach can also help prevent issues such as mold growth and water damage, which can have a negative impact on the health and safety of residents.

AI can also be used to automate routine maintenance tasks, such as HVAC system maintenance, cleaning, and painting. For example, AI-powered systems can be used to schedule routine maintenance tasks based on the needs of the building, the occupancy rate, and other factors. This approach can help public housing authorities reduce the workload on staff, freeing up time for other important tasks. It can also help reduce costs by minimizing the need for manual intervention and improving the efficiency of maintenance operations.

In addition to automating routine maintenance tasks, AI can also be used to enable predictive maintenance. Predictive maintenance involves the use of AI algorithms to analyze data related to building maintenance and identify potential issues before they become major problems. For example, predictive maintenance systems can analyze data related to HVAC systems, plumbing, and other building systems to detect patterns that indicate potential maintenance issues. This approach can help public housing authorities address maintenance issues before they become major problems, reducing costs, and improving the safety and comfort of residents.

Another important application of AI in public housing is in the optimization of energy use. AI can be used to analyze data related to energy consumption in public housing buildings, identify areas where energy is being wasted, and develop strategies to reduce energy use. For example, AI-powered systems can be used to optimize HVAC systems, lighting, and other energy-consuming systems in public housing buildings, reducing energy consumption and lowering costs.

One example of this approach in action is the use of AI-powered energy management systems in public housing buildings. These systems use AI algorithms to analyze data related to energy consumption, identify patterns and trends, and develop strategies to reduce energy use. For example, an energy management system might analyze data related to HVAC use, occupancy rates, and weather patterns to identify opportunities to reduce energy consumption without sacrificing the comfort of residents. This approach can help public housing authorities reduce energy costs, lower carbon emissions, and improve the sustainability of public housing buildings.

In addition to improving maintenance and energy efficiency, AI can also be used to improve the allocation of resources in public housing. By analyzing data related to occupancy rates, resident needs, and other factors, AI algorithms can help public housing authorities develop more effective strategies for allocating resources. For example, AI-powered systems can be used to analyze data related to resident needs, such as healthcare, education, and job training, and develop targeted programs to address these needs. This approach can help public housing authorities better serve the needs of residents, improving their quality of life and reducing the risk of homelessness and other social problems.

One example of this approach in action is the use of AI-powered systems to develop targeted social programs for public housing residents. These systems use AI algorithms to analyze data related to resident needs, such as healthcare, education, and job training, and develop programs to address these needs. For example, a public housing authority might use AI-powered systems to identify residents who are at risk of developing health problems.

In addition to automating routine maintenance tasks, AI can also help public housing authorities optimize their energy use. Energy consumption is a major expense for public housing authorities and reducing energy use can help to lower costs and reduce the carbon footprint of public housing buildings. AI can be used to analyze energy use data and identify areas where improvements can be made. For example, AI algorithms can analyze energy consumption patterns to identify opportunities for energy savings, such as turning off lights and HVAC systems in unoccupied areas.

Another important application of AI in public housing is the use of predictive models to better understand the needs of residents. AI can be used to analyze data related to resident demographics, health, and social needs, and to develop predictive models that can help public housing authorities better understand the needs of residents. This data can be used to allocate resources more effectively, such as providing additional support services to residents with greater needs.

AI can also be used to improve communication and engagement between public housing authorities and residents. For example, AI-powered chatbots can be used to provide residents with 24/7 support and answer common questions about public housing policies and procedures. This can reduce the workload on staff and improve the overall experience of residents.

Despite the many benefits of AI in public housing, there are also challenges that must be addressed. One of the main challenges is the cost of implementing AI systems. Public housing authorities often have limited budgets and investing in AI can be expensive. However, the long-term benefits of AI, such as reduced maintenance costs and improved energy efficiency, can outweigh the initial costs.

Another challenge is the need to ensure that AI systems are transparent and ethical. AI systems must be designed to protect the privacy and security of residents, and to ensure that decisions are made fairly and without bias. There is also a need to ensure that AI systems are accessible to all residents, including those with disabilities or limited digital literacy.

AI has the potential to transform public housing by enabling better management of buildings, reducing maintenance costs, and improving the living conditions of residents. AI can be used to monitor building health and safety, automate routine maintenance tasks, optimize energy use, develop predictive models to better understand resident needs, and improve communication and engagement between public housing authorities and residents. While there are challenges that must be addressed, the benefits of AI in public housing are significant, and continued innovation and investment in this area can help to build a more sustainable and equitable future for all.

Energy Optimization

The potential for AI to optimize energy use in public housing is significant, as reducing energy consumption not only reduces costs but also has a positive impact on the environment. AI can be used to monitor and analyze energy usage data in individual units, enabling public housing authorities to identify areas where energy is being wasted and to take corrective action.

For example, AI-powered sensors can be used to detect whether lights and appliances are being left on when no one is home. This data can then be used to alert residents to turn off appliances or lights, or even automate the process using smart home technology. Additionally, AI can be used to monitor energy usage patterns over time and predict future consumption, allowing for more effective allocation of energy resources.

AI can also be used to optimize energy use across the entire public housing complex. AI algorithms can analyze data related to energy consumption, occupancy, and weather patterns to optimize heating, cooling, and lighting systems. This can help to reduce energy waste and lower utility costs for both public housing authorities and residents.

One example of AI-powered energy optimization in public housing is the use of machine learning algorithms to predict energy consumption patterns. A study by the National Institute of Standards and Technology (NIST) found that machine learning algorithms could accurately predict energy consumption patterns in public housing units, allowing for more effective allocation of energy resources and reducing energy costs.

Another example is the use of smart home technology to optimize energy use. Smart home technology can be used to automate the control of heating, cooling, and lighting systems based on occupancy patterns and weather forecasts. This can help to reduce energy waste and lower utility costs for public housing authorities and residents.

Additionally, AI can be used to identify opportunities for energy-efficient upgrades to public housing buildings. AI algorithms can analyze data related to building materials, insulation, and HVAC systems to identify areas where upgrades could result in significant energy savings. This can help public housing authorities prioritize investments in building upgrades that will have the greatest impact on energy efficiency.

However, there are also challenges associated with the use of AI to optimize energy use in public housing. One challenge is the availability of data. AI algorithms require large amounts of data to be effective, and public housing data is often limited. Additionally, there may be resistance from residents to the installation of sensors and other monitoring devices in their homes.

Another challenge is the cost of implementing AI-powered energy optimization systems. While the long-term cost savings can be significant, there may be high upfront costs associated with the installation of sensors, smart home technology, and other infrastructure needed to support AI-powered energy optimization.

Despite these challenges, the potential benefits of using AI to optimize energy use in public housing are significant. The use of AI-powered sensors and smart home technology can help to reduce energy waste, lower utility costs, and improve the sustainability of public housing. As AI technology continues to advance and become more affordable, it is likely that we will see increased adoption of AI-powered energy optimization in public housing and other types of buildings.

Predictive Analytics

AI has the potential to transform public housing by enabling better management of buildings, reducing maintenance costs, and improving the living conditions of residents. However, perhaps one of the most exciting and promising applications of AI in public housing is the ability to develop predictive models that can help public housing authorities better understand the needs of residents and allocate resources more effectively.

By analyzing data related to resident demographics, health status, and other relevant factors, AI can help public housing authorities identify areas where additional support may be needed. For example, if data analysis shows that a large percentage of residents are struggling with health issues such as asthma or diabetes, public housing authorities could allocate resources to develop programs to address these issues. Alternatively, if data analysis shows that many residents are struggling with unemployment or underemployment, public housing authorities could develop job training and placement programs to help residents find work.

One example of this approach in action is the use of AI-powered systems to develop targeted social programs for public housing residents. These systems use AI algorithms to analyze data related to resident needs, such as healthcare, education, and job training, and develop programs to address these needs. For example, a public housing authority might use AI-powered systems to identify residents who are at risk of developing health problems and develop programs to address these issues, such as providing health screenings, nutrition counseling, or exercise classes.

Another example of the use of predictive models in public housing is the development of algorithms to predict when maintenance issues are likely to arise. By analyzing data related to maintenance issues, such as the age of the building, the type of heating and cooling systems, and the condition of the plumbing and electrical systems, AI algorithms can predict when maintenance issues are likely to occur. This can help public housing authorities schedule maintenance more effectively, reducing the likelihood of costly repairs and ensuring that residents have access to safe and healthy living conditions.

In addition to developing predictive models to improve maintenance and social support, AI can also be used to optimize energy use in public housing, reducing costs and improving sustainability. For example, AI-powered sensors can be used to monitor energy usage in individual units, identifying areas where energy is being wasted. This data can then be used to identify opportunities for energy conservation, such as installing energy-efficient appliances or upgrading insulation. In addition, AI can be used to optimize energy use across the entire public housing complex, ensuring that resources are allocated in the most efficient manner possible.

However, as with any application of AI, there are challenges and limitations that must be addressed in the context of public housing. One of the main challenges is the availability of data. For AI algorithms to be effective, they require large amounts of data to analyze. Unfortunately, public housing authorities often struggle to collect and analyze the data they need to develop effective predictive models. This is partly due to a lack of resources, but it is also due to privacy concerns related to the collection and use of sensitive resident data.

Another challenge is the need for public housing authorities to ensure that the use of AI is ethical and equitable. AI algorithms are only as effective as the data they analyze, and if the data is biased or incomplete, the algorithms will produce biased and incomplete results. This can result in disparities in the allocation of resources and support to residents, perpetuating existing inequalities.

To address these challenges, public housing authorities and AI developers must work together to ensure that AI is used in a way that is ethical, equitable, and effective. This will require investment in data collection and analysis, as well as efforts to address privacy concerns and ensure that AI algorithms are transparent and accountable. It will also require a commitment to addressing issues of bias and inequality, and to ensuring that the benefits of AI are shared equally among all residents of public housing.

Intelligent Resource Allocation

AI has the potential to revolutionize the way public housing authorities allocate resources to better serve residents. By leveraging AI, public housing authorities can gain insights into the needs of residents and identify areas where additional support is required. This can help public housing authorities allocate resources more effectively, reducing costs and improving the quality of life for residents.

One area where AI can be particularly effective in optimizing resource allocation is in the allocation of staff resources. For example, AI algorithms can be used to analyze data related to maintenance requests, identifying areas where additional staff resources are needed. This can help public housing authorities allocate maintenance staff more effectively, reducing response times and improving the overall quality of maintenance services.

AI can also be used to optimize the allocation of social work resources. For example, AI algorithms can be used to analyze data related to the demographics and health status of residents, identifying areas where additional social work support is needed. This data can then be used to allocate social work resources more effectively, ensuring that residents receive the support they need to thrive.

In addition to optimizing resource allocation, AI can also be used to improve the overall efficiency of public housing operations. For example, AI-powered systems can be used to automate routine administrative tasks, such as managing waitlists or processing applications. This can free up staff resources to focus on more complex tasks, such as developing and implementing programs to address resident needs.

One example of this approach in action is the use of AI-powered systems to develop targeted social programs for public housing residents. These systems use AI algorithms to analyze data related to resident needs, such as healthcare, education, and job training, and develop programs to address these needs. For example, a public housing authority might use AI-powered systems to identify residents who are at risk of developing health problems and develop a program to provide additional health education and support.

AI can also be used to optimize energy use in public housing, reducing costs and improving sustainability. For example, AI-powered sensors can be used to monitor energy usage in individual units, identifying areas where energy is being wasted. This data can then be used to identify opportunities for energy conservation, such as installing energy-efficient appliances or upgrading insulation. In addition, AI can be used to optimize energy use across the entire public housing complex, ensuring that resources are allocated in the most efficient manner possible.

However, there are also challenges and limitations associated with the use of AI in public housing. One of the main challenges is the availability of data. AI algorithms require large amounts of data to be effective, and public housing data is often limited. In addition, there are ethical and privacy concerns related to the use of AI in public housing, particularly when it comes to the collection and analysis of sensitive resident data.

Despite these challenges, the potential benefits of using AI in public housing are significant. By leveraging AI to optimize resource allocation, improve operational efficiency, and develop targeted social programs, public housing authorities can improve the quality of life for residents and build more sustainable communities. With continued innovation and investment, AI has the potential to transform public housing and help us build a more equitable and just society.

AI has the potential to transform public housing by enabling better management of buildings, reducing maintenance costs, and improving the living conditions of residents. By leveraging the power of AI, public housing authorities can optimize resource allocation, improve operational efficiency, and enhance the overall quality of housing. However, the implementation of AI in public housing must be done in a responsible and ethical manner, with a focus on transparency and accountability. With continued innovation and investment, AI can help us build more sustainable, efficient, and equitable public housing systems.

Building Monitoring and Maintenance

One of the key challenges facing public housing authorities is maintaining the safety and health of the buildings in their care. Many public housing complexes are older buildings that require regular maintenance to ensure that they remain safe and habitable for residents. However, given the limited resources available to public housing authorities, it can be difficult to conduct maintenance and repairs on a regular basis.

This is where AI comes in. By leveraging the power of AI, public housing authorities can monitor their buildings in real-time, identifying potential issues before they become major problems. AI sensors can be installed throughout the building to detect water leaks, mold, or other hazards that could affect the health of residents. For example, AI-powered humidity sensors can detect when humidity levels rise above a certain threshold, indicating the presence of moisture that could lead to mold growth.

In addition, AI algorithms can be used to detect maintenance issues before they become major problems. For example, AI-powered sensors can detect when HVAC systems are not working properly, indicating the need for maintenance or repair. Similarly, AI algorithms can be used to detect when plumbing systems are not functioning properly, indicating the need for repairs or replacements.

By automating these tasks, public housing authorities can reduce costs, improve response times, and ensure that buildings are safe and healthy for residents. For example, if an AI-powered sensor detects a water leak, it can automatically alert maintenance staff, who can then respond quickly to fix the issue before it causes significant damage.

In addition, AI can be used to optimize maintenance schedules, reducing costs, and minimizing disruption to residents. By analyzing data on the performance of building systems, AI algorithms can identify areas where maintenance is needed and prioritize repairs based on urgency. This can help public housing authorities optimize their maintenance schedules, reducing costs and minimizing disruption to residents.

For example, a public housing authority might use AI to analyze data on the performance of HVAC systems across all its buildings. Based on this analysis, the AI algorithm might identify certain buildings where HVAC systems are more likely to fail and prioritize maintenance in those buildings. This approach can help public housing authorities reduce costs and ensure that maintenance is conducted in a timely and effective manner.

Some examples of local governments using AI for building monitoring and maintenance in public housing. One such example is the New York City Housing Authority (NYCHA), which has implemented an AI-powered system to detect mold in public housing units. The system uses sensors to monitor moisture levels and temperature in apartments, alerting maintenance staff when conditions are conducive to mold growth. This proactive approach has enabled NYCHA to address mold issues before they become major problems, improving the health and safety of residents.

Another example is the Singapore Housing and Development Board (HDB), which has implemented an AI-powered system to monitor the structural integrity of its public housing buildings. The system uses sensors to monitor changes in building structures and identify potential safety hazards. This enables the HDB to take proactive measures to prevent accidents and ensure the safety of residents.

The Los Angeles County Housing Authority (LACHA) has also implemented an AI-powered system for building maintenance. The system uses sensors to monitor building systems, such as heating and cooling, and identify potential maintenance issues. This data is then used to schedule preventative maintenance, reducing the need for costly repairs, and improving the overall efficiency of building maintenance.

The London Borough of Islington has also implemented an AI-powered system for building monitoring and maintenance in its public housing units. The system uses sensors to monitor energy usage, identifying areas where energy is being wasted. This data is then used to develop targeted energy conservation programs, reducing costs, and improving sustainability.

Energy Management

Energy management is an important consideration for public housing authorities, who are often tasked with providing affordable housing to low-income households. In many cases, public housing buildings are older and less energy-efficient than private buildings, which can result in higher energy costs and a larger carbon footprint. However, with the help of AI, public housing authorities can optimize energy use in public housing buildings, reducing costs and making housing more sustainable.

One way that AI can be used to optimize energy use is by monitoring energy consumption patterns in individual units. AI-powered sensors can be installed in public housing units to monitor energy usage, identifying areas where energy is being wasted or where usage can be reduced. For example, an AI system may detect that a resident is leaving lights on during the day or leaving appliances plugged in when not in use. This data can then be used to educate residents on energy-saving behaviors and to make changes to the unit's infrastructure, such as installing more energy-efficient light bulbs or appliances.

AI can also be used to optimize energy use across entire public housing complexes. By analyzing data on occupancy patterns, weather conditions, and other factors, AI algorithms can determine the most efficient way to heat, cool, and light buildings. For example, an AI system may automatically adjust heating and cooling systems based on occupancy patterns, reducing energy consumption when units are unoccupied or adjusting temperatures based on the time of day or weather conditions.

There are many benefits to using AI to optimize energy use in public housing. By reducing energy consumption, public housing authorities can lower energy costs, freeing up resources that can be used to improve housing conditions or provide additional support services to residents. Additionally, by reducing their carbon footprint, public housing authorities can contribute to efforts to combat climate change and create a more sustainable future.

One example of a public housing authority using AI to optimize energy use is the New York City Housing Authority (NYCHA). In 2019, NYCHA launched an Energy Management System (EMS) that uses AI algorithms to optimize energy use in public housing buildings. The EMS is powered by a network of sensors and smart meters that monitor energy usage across NYCHA's portfolio of buildings. The data collected by the sensors is fed into an AI algorithm that determines the most efficient way to heat, cool, and light buildings based on occupancy patterns, weather conditions, and other factors.

The EMS has already led to significant energy savings for NYCHA. According to a report by the Urban Green Council, the

EMS has reduced energy consumption by an average of 8.4% in the buildings where it has been installed. This translates to an annual savings of $4.4 million in energy costs.

Another example of a public housing authority using AI to optimize energy use is the Housing Authority of the City of Pittsburgh (HACP). In 2020, HACP launched an AI-powered energy management platform called ENER-G+. ENER-G+ uses AI algorithms to optimize energy use in public housing buildings by monitoring energy consumption patterns, weather conditions, and other factors. The platform also includes a dashboard that allows building managers to track energy usage and identify areas where energy consumption can be reduced.

According to HACP, ENER-G+ has already led to significant energy savings. In one building, the platform reduced energy consumption by 28%, resulting in an annual savings of $36,000 in energy costs. HACP plans to expand the use of ENER-G+ to additional buildings in the coming years.

Overall, AI has significant potential to optimize energy use in public housing, reducing costs and improving sustainability. By monitoring energy consumption patterns and identifying areas where energy usage can be reduced, public housing authorities can lower energy costs, reduce their carbon footprint, and provide more affordable and sustainable housing to low-income households.

Predictive Analytics

Predictive analytics is an essential tool for public housing authorities to manage resources more effectively. AI algorithms can analyze a vast amount of data related to public housing residents, such as demographic data, income, health status, and education level, among others. This data can then be used to identify patterns and trends, enabling public housing authorities to anticipate future needs and allocate resources accordingly.

One example of this approach in action is the use of predictive analytics to identify which public housing units are likely to need repairs in the future. By analyzing data related to building age, maintenance history, and other factors, AI algorithms can predict which units are likely to need repairs and maintenance soon. This data can be used to schedule repairs and allocate resources more effectively, reducing costs and improving the overall quality of public housing.

Predictive analytics can also be used to identify residents who are at risk of falling behind on rent or facing eviction. By analyzing data related to income, employment status, and other factors, AI algorithms can predict which residents are likely to have difficulty paying rent and provide early intervention to prevent eviction. This approach can reduce the number of evictions, reduce homelessness, and improve the overall stability of public housing communities.

Another example of predictive analytics in public housing is the use of data to identify residents who are at risk of developing health problems. By analyzing data related to health status, lifestyle factors, and demographic data, AI algorithms can predict which residents are at risk of developing chronic diseases such as diabetes, heart disease, or asthma. This data can be used to develop targeted health programs and interventions to improve health outcomes for residents and reduce healthcare costs.

In addition to predictive analytics, AI can also be used to optimize resource allocation in public housing. By analyzing data related to staffing levels, maintenance needs, and other factors, AI algorithms can identify areas where resources are needed and allocate resources more effectively. For example, AI can be used to optimize staffing levels to ensure that there are enough staff members to maintain public housing units and provide support services to residents. This approach can reduce costs and improve the overall quality of public housing.

Another important application of AI in public housing is energy management. AI algorithms can be used to monitor energy consumption patterns and identify areas where energy usage can be reduced. For example, AI can be used to automatically adjust heating and cooling systems based on occupancy patterns, weather conditions, and other factors. By reducing energy consumption, public housing authorities can lower energy costs, reduce their carbon footprint, and make public housing more sustainable.

AI has significant potential to transform public housing by enabling better management of buildings, reducing maintenance costs, and improving the living conditions of residents. By leveraging the power of AI, public housing authorities can optimize resource allocation, improve operational efficiency, and enhance the overall quality of housing. The use of predictive analytics, energy management, and building monitoring and maintenance are just a few examples of how AI can be used in public housing. With continued innovation and investment, AI can help us build more sustainable and equitable public housing communities for all.

Smart Home Technology

Smart home technology has been gaining popularity in recent years, and AI can play a crucial role in its development and implementation in public housing. Smart home technology involves the use of connected devices and sensors that can be controlled through a central system or mobile application. This technology can be used to automate routine tasks, monitor living environments, and provide residents with access to support services.

AI algorithms can be used to analyze data from smart home devices and sensors, enabling public housing authorities to identify areas where improvements can be made. For example, AI can be used to monitor indoor air quality and detect potential health hazards such as high levels of carbon monoxide or allergens. AI can also be used to monitor energy consumption patterns and identify areas where energy usage can be reduced, such as by automatically turning off lights or adjusting heating and cooling systems based on occupancy patterns.

Smart home technology can also be used to provide residents with access to support services such as healthcare, education, and job training. For example, smart home devices can be used to connect residents with healthcare providers or to provide educational resources such as online courses or tutoring services. This can help residents improve their health and well-being, as well as their economic prospects.

One example of smart home technology being implemented in public housing is the work being done by the Housing Authority of the City of Los Angeles (HACLA). HACLA is working with IBM to develop a smart home platform that will allow residents to control their living environments through a mobile application. The platform will also provide residents with access to a range of support services, such as healthcare and education resources.

In addition to improving the living conditions of residents, smart home technology can also have benefits for public housing authorities. By automating routine tasks, such as maintenance and repairs, public housing authorities can reduce costs and improve efficiency. Smart home technology can also help public housing authorities to monitor the health and safety of buildings, ensuring that they are maintained to the highest standards.

Another example of smart home technology being used in public housing is the work being done by the New York City Housing Authority (NYCHA). NYCHA has developed a pilot program that uses smart home devices to monitor the living environments of residents and provide them with access to support services. The program is being implemented in several public housing developments in the city and is designed to improve the health and well-being of residents.

In addition to the benefits of smart home technology, there are also potential risks and challenges that must be addressed. One of the main challenges is ensuring that residents have access to the technology and know how to use it effectively. Public housing authorities may need to provide training and support to residents to ensure that they are able to take advantage of the benefits of smart home technology.

Another challenge is the potential for privacy and security concerns. Smart home devices and sensors collect a significant amount of data about residents and their living environments. Public housing authorities must ensure that this data is collected and used in a responsible and transparent manner, with appropriate safeguards in place to protect residents' privacy and security.

AI has significant potential to transform public housing by enabling better management of buildings, reducing maintenance costs, and improving the living conditions of residents. By leveraging the power of AI, public housing authorities can optimize resource allocation, improve operational efficiency, and enhance the overall quality of housing. Smart home technology has the potential to improve the living conditions of residents by automating routine tasks, monitoring living environments, and providing access to support services. However, public housing authorities must also address the challenges and risks associated with these technologies, ensuring that they are used in a responsible and transparent manner.

Challenges and Limitations

Despite the potential benefits of AI in public housing, there are also challenges and limitations that must be addressed. One of the main challenges is the availability of data. AI algorithms require large amounts of data to be effective, and public housing data is often limited. Additionally, there are ethical and privacy concerns related to the use of AI in public housing. Public housing authorities must ensure that the use of AI is transparent and that the privacy rights of residents are respected.

One way to address the challenge of data availability is to encourage data sharing between public housing authorities and other organizations. For example, public housing authorities could partner with healthcare providers to share data on the health status of residents. This data could then be used to develop predictive models to identify residents who are at risk of developing health problems and allocate resources more effectively.

Another challenge is the ethical and privacy concerns related to the use of AI in public housing. Public housing authorities must ensure that the use of AI is transparent and that the privacy rights of residents are respected. This can be done by developing clear guidelines for the use of AI and ensuring that residents are fully informed about how their data is being used. Additionally, public housing authorities should work with experts in ethics and privacy to ensure that their use of AI is in line with best practices.

One example of a public housing authority addressing these challenges is the New York City Housing Authority (NYCHA). In 2019, NYCHA announced a partnership with Microsoft to develop an AI-powered system to improve the maintenance of its buildings. The system uses sensors and cameras to monitor the health and safety of buildings in real-time, enabling NYCHA to identify and address maintenance issues more quickly. To address privacy concerns, NYCHA developed a set of guidelines for the use of the system, including restrictions on the use of facial recognition technology.

By leveraging the power of AI, public housing authorities can optimize resource allocation, improve operational efficiency, and enhance the overall quality of housing. However, public housing authorities must also address the challenges and limitations of AI, including data availability, ethics, and privacy concerns. With careful planning and attention to these issues, AI can be a powerful tool for improving public housing and enhancing the lives of low-income residents.

Chapter 09: Enhancing Public Education with AI

Education is a fundamental pillar of society and ensuring that every student has access to quality education is crucial for the growth and development of individuals and communities. The traditional model of education, however, has its limitations, with a one-size-fits-all approach that may not cater to the individual needs of students. With the rise of artificial intelligence (AI), there is now an opportunity to leverage this technology to enhance and personalize education for students. AI has the potential to transform the education system by providing tailored learning experiences, identifying at-risk students, and improving teacher training and professional development.

AI-powered Tutoring Systems

Personalized Learning Platforms

AI-powered tutoring systems are becoming increasingly popular in education. These systems use machine learning algorithms to analyze data on student performance and behavior and provide personalized feedback and support. One of the most significant benefits of AI-powered tutoring systems is that they can adapt to each student's unique learning style, strengths, and weaknesses. This level of personalization can help students learn more effectively and achieve better academic outcomes.

Carnegie Learning is an example of an AI-powered tutoring system that is widely used in schools. The system uses cognitive and learning science to provide a personalized learning experience for students. Carnegie Learning's software analyzes data on student performance to identify areas where additional support is needed. The system can then provide immediate feedback and adjust the pace of learning to match the student's needs. By adapting to each student's learning style and progress, Carnegie Learning can help students achieve better outcomes and improve their academic performance.

Another example of an AI-powered tutoring system is Knewton, which uses adaptive learning technology to provide personalized learning experiences for students. Knewton's software analyzes data on student performance and behavior to identify areas where additional support is needed. The system can then provide personalized feedback and adjust the pace of learning to match the student's needs. Knewton's adaptive learning technology has been shown to improve student outcomes in a variety of subjects, including math, science, and language arts.

AI-powered tutoring systems can also be used to provide support for students with special needs. For example, Brain Power's Empower Me program uses AI and augmented reality technology to provide support for students with autism. The program uses a virtual coach to provide personalized feedback and support for students, helping them learn and develop social skills. By leveraging the power of AI, Empower Me can provide a level of support that is not possible with traditional teaching methods.

In addition to AI-powered tutoring systems, AI can also be used to develop personalized learning platforms. These platforms use machine learning algorithms to analyze data on student behavior and performance and provide personalized learning experiences. For example, Edmentum's Exact Path is a personalized learning platform that uses adaptive assessments and learning paths to provide a customized learning experience for each student.

Exact Path analyzes data on student performance to identify areas where additional support is needed. The platform then provides personalized learning paths that adapt to each student's needs and progress. By providing personalized support and feedback, Exact Path can help students achieve better outcomes and improve their academic performance.

Another example of a personalized learning platform is DreamBox Learning, which uses adaptive technology to provide a personalized learning experience for students in math. DreamBox Learning's software analyzes data on student performance to identify areas where additional support is needed. The platform then provides personalized learning experiences that adapt to each student's needs and progress. DreamBox Learning has been shown to improve student outcomes in math and help students develop a love for learning.

AI can also be used to develop predictive analytics tools that can identify at-risk students and provide targeted support. Predictive analytics use machine learning algorithms to analyze data on student performance, behavior, and attendance to identify students who are at risk of falling behind or dropping out. By identifying at-risk students early, schools can provide targeted support to help them stay on track and achieve their academic goals.

For example, the Early Warning System developed by the University of Chicago uses predictive analytics to identify students who are at risk of dropping out. The system analyzes data on student performance, attendance, and behavior to identify students who are at risk. The system then provides targeted support, such as counseling, tutoring, and academic coaching, to help students stay on track and graduate on time.

Another AI-powered tutoring system is Smart Sparrow, which uses adaptive algorithms to personalize learning experiences for students based on their individual needs and learning styles. It also allows educators to create and customize their own courses, making it a versatile tool for personalized learning.

AI-powered tutoring systems have been shown to improve student outcomes, particularly for those who struggle with traditional teaching methods. For example, a study by the National Center for Education

Statistics found that students who used an AI-powered tutoring system called the Cognitive Tutor Algebra I program scored significantly higher on standardized tests than students who received traditional classroom instruction.

In addition to personalized learning, AI can also be used to create more effective assessments. AI algorithms can be used to analyze data from student responses to identify areas where students are struggling and provide targeted support. For example, Edmentum's Study Island is an AI-powered assessment tool that uses machine learning algorithms to analyze student data and provide personalized recommendations for improvement.

AI-powered assessments can also be used to identify areas where curriculum and teaching methods may need to be improved. By analyzing student data, educators can identify gaps in knowledge and areas where students are struggling, allowing them to adjust curriculum and teaching methods accordingly.

Another important application of AI in education is the use of personalized learning platforms. These platforms use AI algorithms to create customized learning experiences for students based on their individual needs and learning styles. For example, DreamBox Learning is an AI-powered platform that adapts to each student's learning style and provides feedback to help students stay on track.

Personalized learning platforms can also be used to track student progress and provide targeted interventions when needed. For example, the Knewton platform uses machine learning algorithms to analyze student data and provide personalized recommendations for improvement. This allows educators to identify at-risk students and provide targeted support before problems escalate.

Predictive analytics is another important application of AI in education. Predictive analytics uses data mining, machine learning, and other AI techniques to analyze student data and identify students who are at risk of dropping out or falling behind. By identifying at-risk students early, educators can provide targeted support and interventions to help these students succeed.

For example, the University of Arizona uses predictive analytics to identify at-risk students and provide targeted support. The university uses a machine learning algorithm to analyze student data, such as grades, attendance, and engagement, to identify students who are at risk of dropping out. The algorithm then recommends interventions, such as tutoring or counseling, to help these students stay on track.

AI can also be used to improve teacher training and professional development. For example, AI-powered tools can be used to analyze teacher performance and provide targeted feedback for improvement. These tools can also be used to identify areas where teachers need additional training or support.

One example of this is the Edthena platform, which uses AI algorithms to analyze teacher performance and provide targeted feedback for improvement. The platform allows teachers to upload videos of their teaching sessions, which are then analyzed by the AI algorithms to identify areas where the teacher can improve. The platform also provides resources for professional development and training based on the areas where the teacher needs improvement.

AI has significant potential to enhance public education in many ways. AI-powered tutoring systems, personalized learning platforms, and predictive analytics can be used to improve student outcomes and identify at-risk students. AI can also be used to create more effective assessments, improve teacher training and professional development, and provide targeted support and interventions for students. With continued investment and innovation, AI has the potential to transform public education and help students achieve their full potential.

Predictive Analytics for At-risk Students

AI-powered predictive analytics can play a significant role in improving student outcomes in education by identifying at-risk students and providing targeted support. Predictive analytics can help educators identify students who are likely to struggle academically, drop out of school, or face other challenges. This data can then be used to provide targeted interventions to help these students succeed.

One example of this is the use of predictive analytics in early warning systems. Early warning systems use predictive analytics to identify students who may be at risk of falling behind academically. These systems analyze data such as attendance, grades, and behavior to identify students who may be struggling. Once identified, these students can receive targeted interventions such as tutoring, mentoring, or academic support to help them stay on track.

Another example of the use of AI in identifying at-risk students is the use of natural language processing (NLP) to analyze student feedback. NLP algorithms can analyze student feedback on assignments, tests, and quizzes to identify areas where students may be struggling or need additional support. This data can then be used to provide targeted feedback and support to help students improve their performance.

AI-powered adaptive learning platforms can also be used to provide personalized learning experiences for students. These platforms use machine learning algorithms to adapt to each student's unique learning style, pace, and level of understanding. Adaptive learning platforms can provide real-time feedback and adjust the difficulty of assignments and assessments to match the student's skill level. This approach can help students learn more effectively and achieve better outcomes.

One example of an AI-powered adaptive learning platform is Knewton, which uses machine learning algorithms to create personalized learning experiences for students. Knewton analyzes student data to identify each student's strengths and weaknesses and adapts its content and assessments to meet their unique needs. Knewton can also provide real-time feedback and insights to help students improve their performance.

AI can also be used to improve teacher training and professional development. AI algorithms can analyze data on teacher performance and provide targeted feedback and support to help teachers improve their effectiveness. For example, AI can be used to analyze classroom data such as student engagement and participation to provide teachers with insights into their teaching practices. This data can then be used to provide targeted feedback and support to help teachers improve their instructional practices.

Another example of the use of AI in teacher training is the use of chatbots. Chatbots can be used to provide teachers with instant access to information and support, such as resources, lesson plans, and instructional strategies. Chatbots can also be used to provide personalized coaching and support to help teachers improve their instructional practices.

Despite the potential benefits of AI in education, there are also challenges and limitations that must be addressed. One of the main challenges is the potential for bias in AI algorithms. AI algorithms are only as good as the data they are trained on, and if the data is biased, the algorithm will be biased as well. For example, if an AI algorithm is trained on data from a particular demographic group, it may not be effective in providing personalized support to students from other demographic groups.

Another challenge is the need for adequate data privacy and security. Education data is sensitive and must be protected from unauthorized access or use. Public trust in AI-powered education systems will depend on the ability of schools and education systems to ensure that student data is kept private and secure.

AI in Teacher Training and Professional

Development

AI can play a significant role in enhancing teacher training and professional development. By analyzing data on teacher performance and student outcomes, AI algorithms can provide personalized recommendations for professional development that can help teachers improve their skills and better support their students.

One example of an AI-powered system for teacher professional development is TeachBoost. TeachBoost uses machine learning algorithms to analyze data on teacher performance, including student outcomes, classroom observations, and self-assessments. Based on this data, TeachBoost provides personalized recommendations for professional development that are tailored to each teacher's needs and goals.

TeachBoost's recommendations can include a variety of professional development activities, such as online courses, workshops, coaching sessions, and peer observations. By providing personalized recommendations, TeachBoost can help teachers improve their skills and knowledge, which can ultimately lead to improved student outcomes.

Another example of AI-powered teacher professional development is the Teacher Advisor with Watson program. This program uses natural language processing and machine learning algorithms to provide teachers with personalized recommendations for lesson planning and classroom instruction. Teachers can input the grade level and subject they are teaching, and the program will provide them with a curated list of resources, including videos, articles, and lesson plans, that are aligned with their specific teaching goals and objectives.

The Teacher Advisor with Watson program also includes a virtual coach feature that allows teachers to ask questions and receive personalized guidance on teaching strategies and classroom management. The virtual coach is powered by IBM's Watson technology, which can understand and respond to natural language questions from teachers.

In addition to providing personalized recommendations for professional development, AI can also be used to analyze and improve teacher performance in the classroom. For example, the Edthena platform uses AI-powered video analysis to provide feedback and coaching to teachers. Teachers can upload videos of their classroom instruction, and the platform will use machine learning algorithms to analyze the video and provide feedback on areas for improvement.

The feedback provided by Edthena is based on research-backed teaching strategies and can help teachers identify areas where they can improve their instructional practices. This feedback can be used to inform professional development activities and improve teacher performance in the classroom.

AI can also be used to improve the evaluation of teacher performance. Traditionally, teacher evaluations have relied on subjective observations by administrators or other evaluators. However, AI can be used to analyze data on teacher performance, such as student outcomes and classroom observations, to provide a more objective evaluation of teacher performance.

One example of an AI-powered teacher evaluation system is the Classroom Snapshot tool. This tool uses machine learning algorithms to analyze data on classroom observations and provide feedback on areas for improvement. The feedback provided by Classroom Snapshot is based on research-backed teaching strategies and can be used to inform professional development activities and improve teacher performance.

In addition to improving teacher training and professional development, AI can also be used to personalize learning experiences for students. AI-powered personalized learning platforms can adapt to students' unique learning styles, strengths, and weaknesses to provide a more effective and engaging learning experience.

One example of an AI-powered personalized learning platform is DreamBox Learning. DreamBox uses machine learning algorithms to adapt to each student's learning needs and provide personalized instruction. The platform provides immediate feedback to students and adjusts the pace and difficulty of instruction based on each student's progress.

Another example of an AI-powered personalized learning platform is Knewton. Knewton uses machine learning algorithms to adapt to each student's learning needs and provide personalized instruction. The platform analyzes data on student performance and provides recommendations for additional resources and activities to support each student's learning.

Challenges and Limitations of AI in Education

The use of artificial intelligence (AI) in education has the potential to revolutionize the way we teach and learn. AI-powered systems can provide personalized learning experiences, identify at-risk students, and enhance teacher training and professional development. However, the use of AI in education also presents several challenges and limitations, including the availability of data and ethical and privacy concerns.

Availability of Data

One of the main challenges of using AI in education is the availability of data. AI algorithms require large amounts of data to be effective, and education data is often limited or difficult to access. For example, data on student performance, attendance, and behavior may be scattered across different systems and difficult to integrate. This can limit the effectiveness of AI-powered systems in providing personalized learning experiences and identifying at-risk students.

To address this challenge, education institutions must invest in data infrastructure and develop systems that can integrate and analyze data from different sources. They must also ensure that data is collected and stored securely and ethically, with appropriate protections for student privacy.

Ethical and Privacy Concerns

Another challenge of using AI in education is the ethical and privacy concerns it raises. AI-powered systems have the potential to collect and analyze large amounts of data on students, including sensitive information such as their personal beliefs and behaviors. This data must be handled with care to avoid compromising student privacy and ensure that it is used ethically.

To address these concerns, education institutions must establish clear policies and guidelines for the use of AI in education. They must ensure that AI-powered systems are transparent and explainable, with clear guidelines for how data is collected, stored, and analyzed. They must also establish clear policies for how data is used and shared and ensure that students and their families are fully informed about how their data is being used.

Examples of AI in Education

Despite these challenges, there are many examples of AI being used to enhance education. Here are a few examples:

1. Personalized Learning Platforms: AI-powered platforms like Dreambox use machine learning algorithms to provide personalized learning experiences for students. These platforms adapt to each student's learning style, strengths, and weaknesses, providing targeted support and feedback.
2. Predictive Analytics: Systems like PAR Framework use predictive analytics to identify at-risk students and provide

targeted interventions. By analyzing data on student performance, attendance, and behavior, these systems can identify students who may be struggling and provide support to help them succeed.

3. Teacher Training and Professional Development: AI-powered systems like TeachBoost provide personalized recommendations for teacher training and professional development. By analyzing data on teaching practices and student outcomes, these systems can provide targeted recommendations for improving teaching practices and better supporting students.

AI has the potential to revolutionize education by providing personalized learning experiences, identifying at-risk students, and enhancing teacher training and professional development. However, there are also challenges and limitations that must be addressed, including the availability of data and ethical and privacy concerns. Education institutions must invest in data infrastructure and establish clear policies and guidelines for the use of AI in education to ensure that it is used ethically and responsibly.

Future of AI in Education

The future of AI in education is promising, with the potential to revolutionize how students learn and teachers teach. As AI technology continues to advance and become more sophisticated, we can expect to see many exciting developments in this field.

One area where we can expect to see significant growth is in the development of AI-powered personalized learning platforms. These platforms will continue to evolve and become even more effective at adapting to each student's unique learning style, strengths, and weaknesses. The platforms will also incorporate more interactive and engaging content, such as virtual and augmented reality, to make learning more immersive and dynamic.

Another area where AI will play a significant role in the future of education is in teacher training and professional development. AI-powered systems can analyze data on teacher performance and student outcomes to provide personalized recommendations for professional development. These recommendations can help teachers improve their teaching practices, better support their students, and ultimately lead to improved student outcomes.

Furthermore, we can expect to see the continued use of predictive analytics to identify at-risk students and provide targeted support. As AI algorithms become even more sophisticated, they will be able to analyze data on student behavior, attendance, and performance to identify potential issues before they become significant problems. This will enable schools to provide timely and effective interventions, such as academic support or counseling, to help at-risk students succeed.

The implementation of AI in education also poses some challenges and limitations that must be addressed. One of the main challenges is the availability of data. AI algorithms require large amounts of data to be effective, and education data is often limited or difficult to access. As such, schools and educational institutions must work to collect and analyze data in a transparent and ethical manner, while also ensuring that student privacy is protected.

Another challenge is ensuring that the use of AI in education is equitable and accessible to all students, regardless of their socioeconomic status or geographical location. Schools must work to bridge the digital divide and ensure that students in underserved communities have access to the technology and resources needed to benefit from AI-powered education.

In addition, there are ethical and social concerns related to the use of AI in education. Some critics argue that AI-powered systems could reinforce existing biases and inequities, and that teachers and human interaction are irreplaceable. Schools and educational institutions must work to ensure that AI is used in a way that is fair, transparent, and accountable.

Advancements in AI for education in the next decade are poised to transform the learning landscape. AI-powered systems have the potential to provide personalized learning experiences for students, support teacher training and professional development, and identify at-risk students for targeted interventions.

According to a Brookings report, AI technologies can unleash the potential and productivity of a huge sector of American and global society, particularly in the education sector. The report notes that AI can provide personalized learning experiences that can improve outcomes for students.

An article from the New York Times highlights how labs are testing AI, virtual reality, and other innovations that could improve learning and lower costs for Generation Z and beyond. The article notes that some of these innovations include AI-powered tutoring systems that can provide immediate feedback and adjust the pace of learning.

A Forbes article predicts that AI and machine learning will transform the scientific method in the next decade, reducing the cost and time required for important science, such as large-scale clinical trials or building particle colliders.

The Pew Research Center notes that some experts predict changes in the overall environment of social media, which could have implications for education in the next decade.

A Forbes Tech Council article predicts that AI has the potential to personalize learning, assess students' progress, and provide real-time feedback, among other applications.

According to the World Economic Forum, almost half of all existing work activities could be automated in the next few decades, including in education. This automation could lead to improved efficiency and lower costs.

Another Brookings report notes that there may be a 10-year implementation lag for AI-related technologies, which means that the full potential of AI in education may not be realized until the next decade.

A TechTalk article notes that AI can be used to personalize learning and assess students' progress, among other applications.

An AI Creations article predicts that AI will continue to transform a range of sectors, including education, over the next decade.

Overall, the future of AI in education is bright, with significant potential to improve student outcomes and enhance the learning experience for students and teachers alike. As AI technology continues to advance and become more sophisticated, we can expect to see many exciting developments in this field, with AI becoming an increasingly integral part of the education system.

Chapter 10: Improving Environmental Sustainability with AI

As we enter a new decade, the need for environmental sustainability has become more pressing than ever. Climate change, deforestation, and pollution are just some of the environmental challenges facing the world today. However, with the advancements in technology, particularly in artificial intelligence (AI), there is now the potential to address these challenges and improve environmental sustainability. In this book, we will explore the ways in which AI can be used to improve environmental sustainability.

What is Environmental Sustainability?

Before diving into the role of AI in environmental sustainability, it is important to first understand what environmental sustainability is and why it is crucial for our planet's future. Environmental sustainability refers to the responsible use and management of natural resources to meet the needs of the present generation without compromising the ability of future generations to meet their own needs. This means that we need to ensure that we are using our natural resources in a way that is not harmful to the environment and that we are doing our best to protect our planet for future generations.

The concept of environmental sustainability has become increasingly important in recent years, as the negative impact of human activities on the environment has become more evident. Climate change, pollution, and deforestation are just some of the many environmental issues that are affecting our planet. These issues can have significant consequences for both the environment and human health, making it crucial to take action to mitigate them.

One of the ways that we can address these environmental issues is using AI. AI has the potential to help us manage our natural resources more efficiently, reduce pollution, and protect our ecosystems. In the following sections, we will explore some of the ways in which AI can be used to improve environmental sustainability.

Optimizing Resource Use

One of the most significant applications of AI in environmental sustainability is in the optimization of resource use. AI algorithms can be used to analyze data on resource use, such as energy consumption or water usage, to identify areas where resources can be used more efficiently. This data can then be used to develop strategies to reduce resource consumption and waste.

For example, AI can be used to optimize energy consumption in buildings by analyzing data on energy usage patterns and identifying areas where energy consumption can be reduced. AI-powered systems can automatically adjust heating and cooling systems based on occupancy patterns and weather conditions to reduce energy consumption. Similarly, AI can be used to optimize water usage by analyzing data on water consumption patterns and identifying areas where water usage can be reduced.

Reducing Pollution

Another important application of AI in environmental sustainability is in the reduction of pollution. AI algorithms can be used to monitor and analyze data on air and water quality to identify sources of pollution and develop strategies to reduce it. For example, AI-powered systems can be used to monitor air quality in urban areas and identify sources of air pollution, such as traffic congestion or industrial emissions. This data can then be used to develop strategies to reduce air pollution, such as implementing traffic restrictions or reducing industrial emissions.

Protecting Ecosystems

AI can also be used to protect ecosystems by monitoring and analyzing data on ecosystems to identify areas that are at risk of degradation or destruction. AI-powered systems can be used to monitor wildlife populations, track deforestation, and detect changes in land use. This data can then be used to develop strategies to protect ecosystems, such as implementing conservation measures or reforestation projects.

For example, the Rainforest Connection uses AI-powered systems to monitor rainforest ecosystems and detect illegal logging activities. The system uses acoustic sensors to detect sounds of chainsaws and trucks, and then sends alerts to park rangers to intervene and prevent the illegal activities.

AI has the potential to be a powerful tool in improving environmental sustainability. From optimizing resource use to reducing pollution and protecting ecosystems, AI can help us manage our natural resources more efficiently and mitigate the negative impact of human activities on the environment. As we continue to face environmental challenges, it is important to explore the potential of AI to help us address them and ensure a sustainable future for generations to come.

How AI can Improve Environmental Sustainability

AI can play a significant role in improving environmental sustainability in various industries. In agriculture, for example, AI can help to monitor and manage environmental conditions to optimize crop production while minimizing negative impacts on the environment. For instance, AI can be used to monitor soil conditions and predict weather patterns to determine the optimal time for planting and harvesting crops. AI can also be used to optimize irrigation systems, reducing water consumption, and preventing overuse of resources.

In transportation, AI can help create more sustainable transportation networks by optimizing routes to reduce fuel consumption, minimizing emissions, and increasing energy efficiency. For instance, AI-powered traffic management systems can analyze real-time data on traffic flows and adjust traffic signals to optimize traffic flows and reduce congestion, which can improve air quality and reduce energy consumption.

AI can also be used in energy management to improve environmental sustainability. AI algorithms can analyze energy consumption patterns and identify areas where energy usage can be reduced. For example, AI can be used to automatically adjust heating and cooling systems in buildings based on occupancy patterns, weather conditions, and other factors. By reducing energy consumption, AI can help lower energy costs, reduce carbon footprints, and make buildings more sustainable.

In waste management, AI can be used to improve recycling and reduce waste. For instance, AI can be used to sort and categorize waste to ensure that recyclable materials are separated and sent for recycling. AI can also be used to optimize waste collection routes, reducing fuel consumption and emissions associated with waste collection.

One example of AI in environmental sustainability is the use of satellite imaging and machine learning algorithms to monitor and manage forests. In Brazil, the Amazon rainforest is home to the largest rainforest in the world and is one of the most biodiverse ecosystems on the planet. However, the Amazon is under threat from deforestation and wildfires, which can have devastating effects on the environment.

To address this issue, a team of researchers used machine learning algorithms to analyze satellite images of the Amazon and identify areas where deforestation was likely to occur. By analyzing historical data on deforestation patterns, the algorithms were able to predict where deforestation was likely to occur in the future and alert authorities to take action to prevent it. This approach has the potential to help prevent environmental disasters and promote sustainable management of natural resources.

Another example of AI in environmental sustainability is the use of predictive analytics to manage water resources. In California, water scarcity is a significant issue, and the state is facing a growing population and increasing water demands. To address this issue, researchers developed a machine learning algorithm that analyzes data on water usage patterns, weather patterns, and other factors to predict future water demand. The algorithm can be used to help water managers make informed decisions about water allocation and conservation, reducing waste and promoting sustainable use of resources.

Overall, AI has the potential to revolutionize environmental sustainability by providing tools to monitor and manage natural resources, optimize processes to minimize environmental impact, and predict and prevent environmental disasters. As AI technology continues to evolve, we can expect to see even more innovative solutions to address the challenges facing our planet.

AI and Agriculture

Agriculture is a significant sector of the global economy, responsible for providing food, fiber, and other materials that are essential to human life. However, the environmental impact of agriculture is also significant, with deforestation, soil degradation, water pollution, and greenhouse gas emissions being major issues. Fortunately, AI has the potential to revolutionize the agriculture industry and make it more sustainable.

One of the ways that AI can be used in agriculture is through precision agriculture techniques. Precision agriculture refers to the use of technology, such as sensors and drones, to monitor and manage crop yields, water usage, and soil health. AI algorithms can analyze data collected from these sensors and provide insights into how to optimize farming practices to reduce environmental impact.

For example, AI-powered sensors can be used to monitor soil moisture levels and adjust irrigation, accordingly, reducing water waste and increasing crop yields. Similarly, drones can be used to collect data on plant health and growth rates, allowing farmers to identify and address issues before they become major problems. AI algorithms can also be used to analyze weather data and predict the optimal times for planting and harvesting crops, reducing waste, and improving efficiency.

Another way that AI can improve environmental sustainability in agriculture is through the development of more sustainable farming practices. For example, AI algorithms can be used to analyze soil health data and recommend ways to improve soil quality, such as by reducing tillage and using cover crops. AI can also be used to optimize the use of fertilizers and pesticides, reducing waste, and minimizing the impact on the environment.

In addition to these applications, AI can also be used to improve the efficiency of food supply chains. AI algorithms can analyze data on transportation routes and shipping methods to reduce the environmental impact of food transportation. For example, AI can identify the most efficient routes and modes of transportation, reducing greenhouse gas emissions and energy consumption.

Overall, AI has the potential to significantly improve the environmental sustainability of the agriculture industry. By providing tools to monitor and manage natural resources, optimize processes to minimize environmental impact, and predict and prevent environmental disasters, AI can help to create a more sustainable food system that meets the needs of the present generation without compromising the ability of future generations to meet their own needs.

AI and Transportation

Transportation is a critical aspect of modern society, allowing people and goods to move around efficiently. However, it also has a significant impact on the environment, with the burning of fossil fuels in vehicles contributing to greenhouse gas emissions and air pollution. Fortunately, AI offers a range of solutions that can help reduce the environmental impact of transportation while maintaining efficiency and convenience.

One way AI can improve transportation is through the optimization of traffic flow. Traffic congestion is a major problem in many urban areas, causing delays, increasing fuel consumption, and contributing to air pollution. AI-powered traffic management systems can monitor traffic patterns, predict congestion, and adjust traffic flow in real-time to reduce congestion and improve efficiency. For example, the city of Barcelona has implemented an AI-powered traffic management system that uses sensors and cameras to monitor traffic flow and adjust traffic lights to optimize traffic flow.

AI can also improve transportation efficiency by optimizing routes and reducing unnecessary travel. For example, logistics companies can use AI-powered route optimization software to minimize the distance and time needed for deliveries, reducing fuel consumption and emissions. Additionally, ride-sharing services such as Uber and Lyft use AI algorithms to match riders with nearby drivers and optimize routes to reduce empty trips and save fuel.

Another way AI can reduce the environmental impact of transportation is by promoting the adoption of electric vehicles (EVs). EVs produce zero emissions, but their adoption has been limited by concerns over range anxiety and charging infrastructure. AI can help address these concerns by providing accurate and real-time information on EV charging station availability and optimizing charging schedules to reduce peak demand and lower electricity costs. For example, Google Maps now includes information on EV charging stations and can even predict how long it will take to charge an EV at a specific station.

In addition to promoting the adoption of EVs, AI can also help improve the efficiency of internal combustion engines (ICEs). One way to do this is by using AI-powered engine management systems that optimize engine performance based on real-time data such as driving conditions and fuel quality. This can lead to significant reductions in fuel consumption and emissions. For example, a study conducted by the University of California, Riverside found that an AI-powered engine management system could improve fuel efficiency by up to 30%.

Finally, AI can be used to reduce the environmental impact of transportation by promoting the adoption of alternative modes of transportation, such as cycling and public transit. AI-powered bike-sharing systems can provide real-time information on bike availability and optimize the distribution of bikes to reduce the need for cars. Public transit systems can also use AI algorithms to optimize routes and schedules, reducing wait times and increasing ridership. For example, the city of Montreal has implemented an AI-powered public transit system that uses real-time data to optimize routes and schedules, leading to a 10% increase in ridership.

AI and Energy

The energy sector is one of the largest contributors to greenhouse gas emissions, responsible for approximately two-thirds of global greenhouse gas emissions. The need to reduce carbon emissions and transition to renewable energy sources is becoming increasingly urgent. The use of artificial intelligence (AI) has the potential to revolutionize the energy sector, from optimizing energy usage to improving the efficiency of energy systems, to developing renewable energy sources. In this chapter, we will explore the potential of AI in the energy sector and its impact on environmental sustainability.

Optimizing Energy Use

One way that AI can help improve environmental sustainability is by optimizing energy use. AI-powered systems can monitor and analyze energy usage data to identify areas of inefficiency and waste. For example, AI algorithms can be used to analyze data from smart meters to identify energy usage patterns and predict future usage. This can help energy providers to adjust their supply to meet demand more efficiently, reducing energy waste and carbon emissions.

AI can also be used to optimize the energy consumption of buildings. Building automation systems can use AI algorithms to control heating, ventilation, and air conditioning (HVAC) systems more efficiently, reducing energy waste while still maintaining comfort levels. AI-powered systems can also analyze data from sensors in buildings to identify areas of energy inefficiency, such as lighting or equipment usage, and make recommendations for improvements.

Improving the Efficiency of Energy Systems

AI can also be used to improve the efficiency of energy systems. For example, AI algorithms can be used to optimize the performance of wind turbines by predicting wind patterns and adjusting turbine settings accordingly. This can improve energy output while reducing the wear and tear on turbines, increasing their lifespan.

AI can also be used to optimize the performance of power grids. Smart grid systems can use AI algorithms to monitor and analyze data from sensors throughout the grid to identify areas of inefficiency or potential failures. This can help energy providers to make proactive adjustments to the grid, reducing the risk of power outages and improving overall efficiency.

Developing Renewable Energy Sources

AI can also be used to help develop renewable energy sources, such as solar and wind power. AI algorithms can be used to optimize the design and placement of solar panels and wind turbines to maximize energy output and efficiency. This can help to reduce the cost of renewable energy while also increasing its availability.

AI can also be used to optimize the storage and distribution of renewable energy. For example, AI algorithms can be used to predict energy usage patterns and adjust the storage and distribution of energy accordingly. This can help to ensure that renewable energy sources are used efficiently and effectively.

Challenges and Limitations

Despite the potential benefits of AI in the energy sector, there are also challenges and limitations that must be addressed. One of the main challenges is the availability and accuracy of data. AI algorithms require large amounts of high-quality data to be effective, and the energy sector often lacks this data. Additionally, there are concerns about the security of energy data and the potential for cyber-attacks on energy systems.

There are also concerns about the ethical implications of using AI in the energy sector. For example, there are concerns about the potential for AI algorithms to be biased or discriminatory. There are also concerns about the impact of AI on jobs in the energy sector, as some tasks may be automated, leading to job losses.

AI and Waste Management

The proper management of waste is essential to ensure environmental sustainability. It is estimated that over 2 billion tons of waste are generated globally every year, and this figure is expected to increase in the future. Poor waste management practices can lead to environmental degradation, including soil and water pollution, air pollution, and the emission of greenhouse gases. Therefore, there is an urgent need to develop innovative solutions to manage waste effectively. One such solution is the application of artificial intelligence (AI) in waste management. In this chapter, we will explore the potential of AI in waste management and its impact on environmental sustainability.

AI in Waste Management

AI can be used to optimize waste management processes and promote recycling and composting. Some of the potential applications of AI in waste management include the following:

1. Smart Waste Management Systems

AI-powered waste management systems can be used to optimize waste collection and transportation processes. These systems can use sensors and real-time data to identify the most efficient routes for waste collection, reducing the time and cost associated with waste collection. For example, the City of Amsterdam has implemented a smart waste management system that uses sensors to monitor waste levels in trash bins, allowing waste collectors to optimize their routes and reduce fuel consumption. Similar systems have been implemented in other cities around the world, including Barcelona, London, and San Francisco.

1. Waste Sorting

AI can also be used to sort waste more efficiently, reducing the amount of waste that ends up in landfills. AI-powered robots can identify and sort different types of waste, including plastics, paper, and metals. These robots use machine learning algorithms to identify the different types of waste and sort them accordingly. For example, AMP Robotics has developed an AI-powered robot that can sort up to 80 items of waste per minute, reducing the need for manual sorting.

1. Recycling

AI can be used to improve the efficiency of recycling processes by identifying materials that can be recycled and developing new recycling technologies. AI-powered systems can identify the types of materials that are present in waste and develop recycling processes that are tailored to these materials. For example, a team of researchers at MIT has developed an AI-powered system that can identify materials that can be recycled from waste and develop recycling processes that are tailored to these materials. This system can help to increase the efficiency of recycling processes and reduce the amount of waste that ends up in landfills.

1. Composting

AI can also be used to promote composting, which is an environmentally friendly way of managing organic waste. Composting involves the natural breakdown of organic waste, such as food waste and yard waste, into nutrient-rich soil that can be used to fertilize plants. AI-powered systems can be used to monitor composting processes and optimize them for maximum efficiency. For example, the City of San Francisco has implemented an AI-powered system that uses sensors to monitor composting processes and optimize them for maximum efficiency. Similar systems have been implemented in other cities around the world, including Paris and Toronto.

The application of AI in waste management can have a significant impact on environmental sustainability. By optimizing waste collection and transportation processes, AI-powered waste management systems can reduce the amount of fuel consumed by waste collection vehicles, leading to a reduction in greenhouse gas emissions. By sorting waste more efficiently, AI-powered robots can reduce the amount of waste that ends up in landfills, leading to a reduction in greenhouse gas emissions and the preservation of natural resources. By improving the efficiency of recycling processes, AI-powered systems can reduce the amount of waste that ends up in landfills and promote the use of recycled materials, leading to a reduction in greenhouse gas emissions and the preservation of natural resources. By promoting composting, AI-powered systems can reduce the amount of organic waste that ends up in land

Challenges and Limitations of AI in Environmental Sustainability

The use of AI in environmental sustainability has the potential to revolutionize the way we manage and protect our natural resources. However, as with any emerging technology, there are challenges and limitations that must be addressed. In this chapter, we will explore some of the challenges and limitations of AI in environmental sustainability and discuss possible solutions.

Limited Data Availability

One of the main challenges of using AI in environmental sustainability is the availability of data. AI algorithms require large amounts of data to be effective, and environmental data can be limited or difficult to access. For example, data on deforestation rates in remote areas of the Amazon rainforest may not be readily available. This can make it difficult to develop effective AI models for managing and protecting natural resources.

However, there are solutions to this challenge. One solution is to develop partnerships with organizations that have access to the data. For example, government agencies, research institutions, and non-governmental organizations (NGOs) may have access to data that can be used to develop effective AI models. Additionally, the use of remote sensing technologies, such as satellites, can provide valuable data on environmental conditions in remote areas.

Ethical and Privacy Concerns

Another challenge of using AI in environmental sustainability is the potential for ethical and privacy concerns. For example, the use of AI in monitoring and surveillance of natural resources may raise concerns about privacy and data protection. Additionally, there may be concerns about the use of AI in decision-making processes related to environmental policies.

To address these concerns, it is important to ensure that the use of AI in environmental sustainability is transparent, fair, and does not compromise privacy. This can be done by developing clear guidelines for the use of AI in environmental sustainability and ensuring that stakeholders are aware of the data being collected and how it is being used.

Unintended Consequences

Another challenge of using AI in environmental sustainability is the potential for unintended consequences. For example, optimizing energy use in one area may lead to increased energy use in another area, or reducing waste in one area may lead to increased waste in another area.

To address these unintended consequences, it is important to take a holistic approach to environmental sustainability. This involves considering the potential impacts of AI on the environment, rather than focusing on specific areas or issues. Additionally, it is important to involve stakeholders in the development and implementation of AI models to ensure that their concerns and perspectives are considered.

Case Studies in AI and Environmental Sustainability

In recent years, artificial intelligence (AI) has shown great potential in improving environmental sustainability in various industries such as agriculture, transportation, energy, and waste management. This section will provide modern case studies of how AI is being used to address environmental challenges and improve sustainability in these industries.

Agriculture

WildTrack is an environmental organization that specializes in non-invasive wildlife monitoring using AI to improve their footprint-gathering technique. Their approach is to use advanced data analytics, artificial intelligence, and traditional ecological knowledge to protect endangered species. WildTrack's Footprint Identification Technique (FIT) is a tool for non-invasive monitoring of endangered species through digital images of footprints. The measurements from these images are analyzed by customized mathematical models that help to identify the species, individual, sex, and age-class. By using AI, WildTrack has been able to re-create indigenous animal-tracking skills at scale, which enables them to monitor wildlife populations more efficiently and effectively, without disturbing their normal behavior, ecology, or physiology.

In addition to wildlife monitoring, AI is also being used to optimize farming practices in agriculture. For example, Farmers Edge is a company that uses AI-powered analytics to help farmers optimize crop yields and reduce waste by providing insights into soil health and moisture levels. By using precision agriculture techniques, AI can monitor and manage crop yields, water usage, and soil health, thus reducing environmental impact. Through AI, Farmers Edge can provide farmers with customized recommendations to increase crop yields, reduce input costs, and minimize environmental impact.

WildTrack and Farmers Edge are examples of how AI is being used to improve environmental sustainability in various industries. By using AI to monitor wildlife populations, WildTrack is helping to protect endangered species while minimizing disturbance to their natural habitat. By using AI in precision agriculture, Farmers Edge is helping to optimize crop yields and reduce waste while minimizing environmental impact. These case studies demonstrate how AI can be used to address environmental challenges and improve sustainability in various industries.

Transportation

Greenhouse gas emissions from the transportation sector contribute significantly to anthropogenic greenhouse gas emissions in the United States, making it the largest contributor of U.S. greenhouse gas emissions. To address this issue, AI can be used to optimize transportation networks, reduce congestion, and improve the efficiency of transport systems.

Optibus is a company that uses AI to optimize public transportation networks, reduce fuel consumption, and improve the reliability of public transportation. Their platform uses real-time data from transportation networks to improve operational efficiency by optimizing the use of vehicles and drivers, predicting demand, and reducing the time spent on waiting for passengers. By optimizing transportation routes and reducing fuel consumption, companies like Optibus can significantly reduce the greenhouse gas emissions associated with transportation.

Another example of AI being used to address transportation-related greenhouse gas emissions is the Smart Mobility system. The system uses AI to optimize traffic flow in urban areas, reduce congestion, and improve air quality. The system collects data from various sources, such as GPS and traffic sensors, to create real-time traffic models. These models are used to optimize traffic flow by adjusting traffic signal timings and rerouting traffic in congested areas. The system has been shown to reduce travel time, improve fuel efficiency, and reduce greenhouse gas emissions.

Energy

The energy sector is a significant contributor to greenhouse gas emissions, responsible for over two-thirds of global emissions attributed to human activity. In the United States, including direct and indirect emissions associated with electricity use, the industry's share of total greenhouse gas emissions in 2021 was 30%, the largest of any sector.

However, AI has the potential to significantly reduce greenhouse gas emissions from the energy sector by optimizing energy use, improving the efficiency of energy systems, and developing renewable energy sources. For instance, DeepMind, a company that specializes in artificial intelligence, has developed an AI system that reduced the amount of energy used for cooling data centers by up to 40%. Ecovat is another company that uses AI to optimize energy storage systems, which reduces the reliance on non-renewable energy sources.

It is important to note that reducing greenhouse gas emissions in the energy sector is crucial for addressing climate change. The energy supply sector, which includes electricity, heat, and other energy, is the largest contributor to global greenhouse gas emissions, responsible for about 35% of total emissions. Therefore, the use of AI in the energy sector can play a significant role in mitigating climate change.

Waste Management

Waste management is an essential component of environmental sustainability. Artificial intelligence (AI) is increasingly being used to optimize waste management processes, reduce waste, and promote recycling and composting. For example, GreenQ is a waste management company that uses AI to optimize waste collection routes by analyzing data from sensors in waste bins and predicting their fill levels. By doing so, GreenQ can reduce fuel consumption, improve the efficiency of waste collection, and lower costs. Another company, AMP Robotics, uses AI to sort and recycle waste, improving recycling rates and reducing the amount of waste that ends up in landfills.

In addition to these two examples, AI has the potential to transform the entire waste management industry. Waste management companies can use AI technologies to monitor the fullness of waste containers across the city and optimize waste collection time, routes, and frequencies. This optimization enhances the rapidity at which waste bins are collected and prevents overflowing, ultimately reducing waste in landfills. Moreover, AI technologies can assist in detecting, predicting, and incentivizing environmental transitions, leading to early detection of big and small transitions with potentially significant ripple effects. Robotics, coupled with AI and machine learning, can also improve the quality of the waste management process as it becomes more complex, and health conditions for workers, especially in handling medical and biohazardous waste.

The Future of AI and Environmental Sustainability

The potential applications of AI in environmental sustainability are vast and diverse. As technology continues to advance, we can expect to see even more innovative solutions that leverage AI to address some of the biggest environmental challenges facing the world today. Here are some examples of how AI is being used in environmental sustainability:

1. Monitoring and managing ocean health: AI systems can be used to analyze data collected from sensors and satellites to identify patterns and changes in ocean temperature, acidity levels, and other important metrics. This information can then be used to guide conservation efforts, such as identifying areas that are particularly vulnerable to pollution or overfishing.

2. Improving energy efficiency: AI can be used to optimize energy usage in buildings and transportation systems, reducing greenhouse gas emissions and saving money. For example, AI-powered algorithms can analyze energy consumption patterns to identify opportunities for optimization and adjust in real-time.

3. Enhancing precision agriculture: AI-powered sensors can collect data on soil quality, moisture levels, and plant health, allowing farmers to make data-driven decisions about planting, fertilization, and irrigation. This can help reduce waste and improve crop yields, while also minimizing the use of pesticides and other harmful chemicals.

4. Combating deforestation: AI systems can be used to monitor forests in real-time, identifying areas where deforestation is occurring and alerting authorities to act. This can help prevent illegal logging and protect critical habitats for endangered species.

5. Predicting and mitigating natural disasters: AI can be used to analyze data from weather satellites, sensors, and social media to predict the likelihood and severity of natural disasters such as hurricanes and floods. This information can then be used to develop early warning systems and evacuation plans, saving

lives, and minimizing damage.

6. Improving air and water quality: AI can be used to monitor air and water quality in real-time, identifying sources of pollution and helping to develop strategies to reduce emissions and improve water treatment. For example, AI-powered sensors can be used to monitor pollution levels in cities and adjust traffic flow to reduce emissions.

7. Designing sustainable infrastructure: AI can be used to design and optimize low-emission transportation networks, energy-efficient buildings, and sustainable cities. For example, AI-powered simulations can be used to optimize traffic flow, reducing congestion and emissions.

8. Managing waste: AI can be used to optimize waste management systems, reducing the amount of waste generated and improving recycling rates. For example, AI-powered sensors can be used to identify recycling contamination and optimize waste collection routes.

Overall, the potential applications of AI in environmental sustainability are vast and varied. From monitoring ocean health to predicting and mitigating natural disasters, AI has the power to transform the way we address some of the biggest environmental challenges facing the world today. As technology continues to advance, we can expect to see even more innovative solutions that leverage AI to address some of the biggest environmental challenges facing the world today.

Chapter 11: Enhancing Tourism with AI

Tourism is a vital industry for many countries, contributing significantly to their economic growth and providing employment opportunities for local communities. With the rise of artificial intelligence (AI), there is an opportunity to enhance the tourism experience for visitors and increase the efficiency of tourism operations. In this book, we will discuss the use of AI-powered tourism platforms, personalized recommendations for visitors, and real-time translation services. We will also explore the use of AI in tourism marketing and advertising.

AI-powered Tourism Platforms

AI-powered tourism platforms have revolutionized the way visitors plan their trips and experience destinations. These platforms leverage machine learning algorithms to analyze vast amounts of data, including visitor reviews, social media posts, search queries, and more, to provide personalized recommendations for accommodations, attractions, and activities. By tailoring recommendations based on individual preferences and past behavior, AI-powered tourism platforms can enhance the overall visitor experience.

One notable example of an AI-powered tourism platform is Booking.com[1]. The travel booking website uses AI to provide personalized recommendations for accommodations based on a visitor's search history and preferences. For instance, if a visitor frequently books budget-friendly accommodations, the platform will recommend similar options in the future. Additionally, Booking.com[2] uses AI to analyze visitor reviews and ratings, allowing the platform to suggest properties that are more likely to meet a visitor's expectations.

---

1.   http://booking.com/

2.   http://booking.com/

Another example of an AI-powered tourism platform is Utrip. This travel planning platform uses machine learning algorithms to recommend personalized itineraries based on a visitor's interests, travel dates, and budget. The platform analyzes data from various sources, such as visitor reviews, social media posts, and travel blogs, to make recommendations for attractions, restaurants, and activities. By using AI to tailor recommendations to individual visitors, Utrip aims to provide a more seamless and enjoyable trip planning experience.

Aside from enhancing the visitor experience, AI-powered tourism platforms can also improve the efficiency of tourism operations. The tourist information center in Helsinki, Finland, for example, uses an AI-powered chatbot to provide visitors with information about the city. The chatbot can answer common questions, such as "What are the best restaurants in Helsinki?" or "How do I get to the airport?" This allows the tourist information center staff to focus on more complex inquiries and provide a better overall experience for visitors.

Similarly, AI-powered chatbots can also be used by hotels and resorts to provide quick and efficient customer service. For example, Marriott International uses an AI-powered chatbot named "ChatBotlr" to assist guests with room service orders, housekeeping requests, and other common inquiries. The chatbot is available 24/7 and can be accessed through a guest's mobile device or computer.

AI-powered tourism platforms can also be used to improve accessibility for visitors with disabilities. The travel planning platform, AccessNow, uses AI to provide personalized recommendations for accessible accommodations, restaurants, and attractions. The platform allows visitors to filter search results by specific accessibility features, such as wheelchair ramps or hearing loops, and uses machine learning algorithms to suggest options that best meet their needs.

Moreover, AI-powered translation services can enhance the experience of international visitors who may not be fluent in the local language. For example, Google Translate uses AI to provide real-time translations of text and speech in over 100 languages. Visitors can use the app to translate menus, signs, and other written text, as well as to communicate with locals through speech translation.

In addition to enhancing the visitor experience, AI can also be used in tourism marketing and advertising. For example, the travel company, Expedia, uses AI to analyze data from visitor searches and clicks to optimize its advertising campaigns. The platform uses machine learning algorithms to identify patterns in visitor behavior, such as preferred destinations or travel dates, and adjusts its advertising strategy accordingly.

Similarly, AI-powered chatbots can be used for targeted marketing campaigns. The chatbot can be programmed to ask visitors about their interests and preferences and use that information to suggest personalized recommendations for attractions, accommodations, and activities. This can be especially useful for destinations that are lesser-known or have niche offerings.

Personalized Recommendations for Visitors

Personalized recommendations can significantly enhance the tourism experience for visitors. AI can be used to provide recommendations based on a visitor's preferences, such as their favorite types of food, activities, and attractions. For example, the travel website TripAdvisor uses AI to provide personalized recommendations for hotels, restaurants, and attractions based on a visitor's search history and preferences.

AI can also be used to provide personalized recommendations for activities and experiences. For example, the AI-powered travel platform Klook uses machine learning algorithms to recommend personalized experiences based on a visitor's interests, travel dates, and budget. The platform analyzes data from various sources, such as visitor reviews, social media posts, and travel blogs, to make recommendations for activities, tours, and attractions.

Personalized recommendations can also help visitors discover new experiences and attractions that they might not have otherwise found. For example, the travel planning platform GetYourGuide uses AI to recommend personalized tours and activities based on a visitor's preferences and past behavior. The platform can recommend tours and activities that are off the beaten path and not typically recommended by travel guidebooks or tour operators.

Chapter 3: Real-time Translation Services

Real-time translation services can significantly enhance the tourism experience for visitors who do not speak the local language. AI can be used to provide real-time translation services for visitors, allowing them to communicate with locals and navigate the city more easily. For example, the Google Translate app uses AI to provide real-time translation services for over 100 languages.

Real-time translation services can also improve the efficiency of tourism operations. For example, the tourist information center in Tokyo, Japan, uses an AI-powered translation device to communicate with visitors who do not speak Japanese. The device can translate between Japanese and multiple languages, including English, Chinese, and Korean, allowing the tourist information center staff to provide better service to visitors.

Personalized Recommendations for Visitors

One of the most exciting potential applications of AI in tourism is the ability to provide personalized recommendations for visitors. By analyzing a visitor's preferences, behaviors, and past interactions, AI-powered systems can generate personalized recommendations for things to do, places to visit, and experiences to have during their trip. This can help visitors make the most of their time and have a more enjoyable experience overall.

One example of a company using AI for personalized recommendations is Airbnb. The company's AI-powered system uses data from user searches, bookings, and reviews to generate personalized recommendations for accommodations and experiences. The system also considers factors such as the traveler's budget, location preferences, and travel dates to provide the most relevant recommendations.

In addition to accommodations and experiences, AI-powered systems can also generate personalized recommendations for dining and shopping. For example, the app MyTi can recommend restaurants based on a user's preferences and past dining experiences, and the app Hopper can recommend shopping destinations based on a user's interests.

Real-Time Translation Services

Another area where AI can enhance the tourism experience is in real-time translation services. Language barriers can be a major hurdle for international travelers, but AI-powered translation systems can help break down these barriers and facilitate communication between travelers and locals.

One example of a company using AI for real-time translation is Google. The company's Google Translate app uses AI to translate text and speech in real-time, allowing travelers to communicate with locals even if they don't speak the same language. The app can also translate signs and menus, making it easier for travelers to navigate and order in restaurants and stores.

Another example is the translation earpiece by Waverly Labs, which uses AI to translate speech in real-time. The earpiece works by detecting speech from the speaker and translating it into the listener's language, and vice versa. This technology can be especially useful for international business travelers and tourists.

AI in Tourism Marketing and Advertising

Finally, AI can also be used in tourism marketing and advertising to reach potential visitors and provide them with targeted, personalized content. By analyzing data on a visitor's preferences, behaviors, and past interactions, AI-powered systems can generate personalized marketing content that is more likely to resonate with the visitor.

One example of a company using AI in tourism marketing is Visit Orlando, which used an AI-powered platform to target potential visitors with personalized ads. The platform analyzed data on user behavior and interests to provide customized ads that were more likely to result in bookings.

Another example is the AI-powered chatbot by Visit Tallinn, which provides visitors with personalized recommendations for things to do and see in Tallinn. The chatbot uses natural language processing and machine learning to understand the visitor's preferences and provide tailored recommendations.

AI has the potential to revolutionize the tourism industry by enhancing the visitor experience, facilitating communication, and improving marketing and advertising efforts. From AI-powered tourism platforms to real-time translation services, the applications of AI in tourism are numerous and varied. As technology continues to advance, we can expect to see even more innovative solutions that leverage AI to enhance the tourism experience and drive economic growth for local governments.

Chapter 12: Improving Civic Engagement with AI

Civic engagement is crucial for the success and sustainability of a democracy. It is the active participation of citizens in the democratic process, such as voting, communicating with elected officials, participating in community events, and volunteering for campaigns or political organizations. In recent years, advancements in artificial intelligence (AI) have opened new possibilities for civic engagement. AI-powered platforms can help increase citizen participation and improve the accuracy of public opinion polling and election forecasting. In this chapter, we will explore the use of AI in enhancing civic engagement in local communities.

AI-powered platforms for citizen feedback and engagement

One of the most promising applications of AI in civic engagement is the development of AI-powered platforms for citizen feedback and engagement. These platforms use machine learning algorithms to analyze large volumes of citizen feedback, such as emails, social media posts, and phone calls, to identify common concerns and issues in a community.

One example of an AI-powered platform for citizen feedback and engagement is the CityVoice platform. CityVoice uses natural language processing (NLP) and machine learning algorithms to analyze citizen feedback from various sources, such as social media, email, and phone calls, to provide real-time insights into citizen concerns and issues. The platform can also categorize feedback by issue area and location, making it easier for local officials to prioritize and address citizen concerns.

Another example of an AI-powered platform for citizen engagement is the Speak Up! app. The app uses machine learning algorithms to analyze citizen feedback and provide personalized recommendations for how citizens can get involved in local government. For example, if a citizen expresses concern about a particular issue, such as affordable housing, the app may recommend that they attend a local government meeting or contact their elected officials to voice their concerns.

The use of AI in public opinion polling

Another way in which AI can enhance civic engagement is through its use in public opinion polling. Traditional public opinion polling methods, such as phone surveys, can be expensive and time-consuming, and may not accurately capture the views of all members of a community. AI-powered polling methods can help address these issues by analyzing large volumes of social media data to identify trends and patterns in public opinion.

One example of an AI-powered public opinion polling method is the use of sentiment analysis. Sentiment analysis uses NLP and machine learning algorithms to analyze social media data and determine the sentiment, or emotional tone, of a particular topic or issue. This can help provide a more accurate picture of public opinion on a particular issue.

Another example of an AI-powered public opinion polling method is the use of predictive analytics. Predictive analytics uses machine learning algorithms to analyze data from past elections and public opinion polls to forecast future election results. This can help campaigns and political organizations better target their outreach efforts and increase voter engagement.

The use of AI in election forecasting

Finally, AI can also be used to enhance election forecasting. AI-powered election forecasting methods use machine learning algorithms to analyze large volumes of data, such as past election results, polling data, and demographic data, to predict the outcome of an election.

One example of an AI-powered election forecasting method is the use of deep learning algorithms. Deep learning algorithms use neural networks to analyze large volumes of data and identify patterns and trends. This can help predict the outcome of an election with greater accuracy than traditional polling methods.

Another example of an AI-powered election forecasting method is the use of predictive analytics. Predictive analytics uses machine learning algorithms to analyze past election results and identify key factors that may influence future election outcomes. This can help political organizations and campaigns better target their outreach efforts and increase voter engagement.

Civic engagement is a critical component of a thriving democracy, and advancements in artificial intelligence (AI) have opened new possibilities for enhancing civic engagement in local communities. AI-powered platforms can help increase citizen participation and improve the accuracy of public opinion polling and election forecasting.

AI-powered platforms for citizen feedback and engagement use machine learning algorithms to analyze large volumes of citizen feedback from various sources such as social media, email, and phone calls, to identify common concerns and issues in a community. For instance, CityVoice and Speak Up! are AI-powered platforms that use natural language processing (NLP) and machine learning algorithms to provide real-time insights into citizen concerns and issues, as well as categorize feedback by issue area and location. This makes it easier for local officials to prioritize and address citizen concerns.

The use of AI in public opinion polling is another way in which AI can enhance civic engagement. Traditional polling methods can be expensive and time-consuming and may not accurately capture the views of all members of a community. However, AI-powered polling methods can analyze large volumes of social media data using sentiment analysis and predictive analytics to identify trends and patterns in public opinion. This can provide a more accurate picture of public opinion on a particular issue.

Finally, AI can also be used to enhance election forecasting. AI-powered election forecasting methods use machine learning algorithms to analyze large volumes of data, such as past election results, polling data, and demographic data, to predict the outcome of an election. Deep learning algorithms and predictive analytics are two examples of AI-powered election forecasting methods that can predict the outcome of an election with greater accuracy than traditional polling methods.

Chapter 13: Enhancing Accessibility with AI

Accessibility is an important issue for local governments, as it directly impacts the quality of life of citizens with disabilities. Despite various efforts to improve accessibility, there are still many challenges faced by people with disabilities in accessing public spaces, services, and information. However, recent advancements in artificial intelligence (AI) have opened new possibilities for enhancing accessibility. AI-powered systems can help to provide real-time translation, captioning, and audio descriptions to enable people with disabilities to access information and services more easily. In this chapter, we will explore the use of AI-powered systems for sign language interpretation, real-time captioning, and audio descriptions. We will also discuss the use of AI in accessibility planning and design.

AI-powered Systems for Sign Language Interpretation

Sign language interpretation is a crucial service that enables people with hearing disabilities to communicate effectively and access information. However, the availability and cost of sign language interpreters can be significant barriers for many individuals. Advancements in artificial intelligence (AI) have opened new possibilities for real-time sign language interpretation using computer vision and natural language processing technologies.

One of the most promising AI-powered sign language interpretation systems is SignAll. SignAll uses a combination of computer vision and machine learning algorithms to interpret sign language in real-time. The system can translate sign language into written text, spoken language, or other forms of communication. This enables people with hearing disabilities to communicate with others more easily and access information in real-time.

SignAll's technology is based on a combination of computer vision, machine learning, and natural language processing. The system uses cameras to capture the user's sign language movements and then uses computer vision algorithms to interpret those movements. The system can recognize a wide range of sign language gestures, including complex grammatical structures and nuances of meaning. Once the sign language is interpreted, the system can translate it into written text, spoken language, or other forms of communication, depending on the user's preferences.

SignAll's technology has been tested in a variety of settings, including classrooms, workplaces, and public events. In one case study, SignAll was used to provide real-time sign language interpretation at a conference for people with hearing disabilities. The system was able to interpret a wide range of sign language gestures and translate them into written text for participants to read on a screen. This enabled participants to follow the presentations and discussions more easily and participate more fully in the event.

Another example of an AI-powered sign language interpretation system is VL2SignPrime. VL2SignPrime uses a combination of computer vision and machine learning algorithms to recognize and interpret American Sign Language (ASL) in real-time. The system can translate ASL into written text or spoken language, allowing people with hearing disabilities to communicate more easily with others.

VL2SignPrime's technology is based on a deep learning algorithm that has been trained on a large dataset of ASL videos. The system uses computer vision to recognize the user's sign language gestures and then uses the deep learning algorithm to interpret those gestures. Once the sign language is interpreted, the system can translate it into written text or spoken language using text-to-speech or speech-to-text technology.

VL2SignPrime has been tested in a variety of settings, including classrooms and video conferencing. In one case study, VL2SignPrime was used to provide real-time sign language interpretation during a video conference between a deaf individual and a hearing individual. The system was able to recognize and interpret the sign language gestures in real-time, allowing the deaf individual to communicate more effectively with the hearing individual.

AI-powered sign language interpretation systems have the potential to significantly improve accessibility for people with hearing disabilities. These systems can provide real-time interpretation that is more accurate and cost-effective than traditional sign language interpretation services. They can also be customized to meet the specific needs and preferences of individual users, enabling them to communicate more effectively and access information in real-time.

However, there are also some limitations and challenges associated with AI-powered sign language interpretation systems. For example, these systems may struggle to interpret sign language in low-light conditions or when there are multiple people signing at the same time. They may also struggle to interpret certain nuances of meaning or regional variations in sign language. Additionally, some individuals may prefer traditional sign language interpretation services that provide a more personal and human touch.

AI-powered Systems for Real-time Captioning

Real-time captioning is an important accessibility service for people with hearing disabilities, as it enables them to follow spoken language in real-time. However, traditional captioning services can be expensive and require a significant amount of time and effort to produce. AI-powered systems can help to overcome these challenges by providing real-time captioning using speech recognition and natural language processing technologies.

Speech recognition technology has come a long way in recent years, and AI-powered systems are now capable of accurately transcribing spoken language in real-time. These systems use machine learning algorithms to analyze audio input and convert it into text, which can then be displayed as captions. Real-time captioning can be particularly useful in situations such as live events, conferences, and public meetings, where it may be difficult or impossible to provide traditional captioning services.

One example of an AI-powered real-time captioning system is Ava. Ava uses a combination of speech recognition and machine learning algorithms to provide real-time captions for conversations and events. The system can be used on smartphones, tablets, and other mobile devices, enabling people with hearing disabilities to access real-time captioning in any situation. Ava's speech recognition technology is designed to be highly accurate, even in noisy environments, and the system can also recognize multiple speakers and distinguish between them.

Another example of an AI-powered real-time captioning system is Google's Live Caption. Live Caption uses speech recognition and machine learning algorithms to provide real-time captions for videos and audio content on Android devices. The system can caption any media playing on the device, including videos, podcasts, and even phone calls. Live Caption is designed to be easy to use and can be enabled with a single tap.

AI-powered real-time captioning systems can also be integrated into existing communication platforms, such as Zoom and Microsoft Teams, to provide real-time captions for video conferences and meetings. Microsoft Teams, for example, offers a live caption feature that uses AI-powered speech recognition to provide real-time captions during meetings. This feature can be particularly useful for people with hearing disabilities who may struggle to follow the conversation in a group setting.

AI-powered real-time captioning systems can also be used to provide accessibility for online content, such as videos and webinars. For example, YouTube offers automatic captioning for videos using its own AI-powered speech recognition technology. While the accuracy of automatic captioning can vary depending on the quality of the audio input, it can still be a valuable tool for people with hearing disabilities who may not have access to traditional captioning services.

In addition to providing real-time captioning, AI-powered systems can also be used to generate captions for pre-recorded content. For example, IBM's Watson Captioning service uses speech recognition and natural language processing technologies to provide accurate and timely captions for pre-recorded video content. The system is designed to be highly accurate and can also recognize and transcribe multiple speakers.

Overall, AI-powered real-time captioning systems have the potential to greatly improve accessibility for people with hearing disabilities. By using advanced speech recognition and machine learning algorithms, these systems can provide accurate and timely captions in a variety of settings, from live events and meetings to online content and pre-recorded videos. As technology continues to improve, we can expect to see even more innovative solutions for real-time captioning and accessibility in the future.

AI-powered Systems for Audio Descriptions

Audio descriptions are an essential accessibility service for people with visual disabilities, as they provide a verbal description of visual content such as movies, TV shows, and live events. Audio descriptions can help people with visual disabilities to understand the plot, characters, setting, and other details of visual content that they may not be able to see. However, the availability of audio descriptions can be limited, and producing them can be time-consuming and expensive. AI-powered systems can help to overcome these challenges by providing real-time audio descriptions using computer vision and natural language processing technologies.

One of the most significant advantages of AI-powered audio description systems is their ability to provide real-time audio descriptions. Traditional audio description methods require pre-recording descriptions that are later synchronized with the visual content. This process can be time-consuming and may result in delays in making audio descriptions available to the audience. In contrast, AI-powered audio description systems can generate descriptions in real-time, enabling people with visual disabilities to access audio descriptions in any situation.

The Audio Description Project is an example of an AI-powered audio description system that uses a combination of computer vision and machine learning algorithms to provide real-time audio descriptions for movies, TV shows, and other visual content. The system uses computer vision algorithms to analyze the visual content and identify key elements such as characters, settings, and actions. The system then generates a natural language description of the visual content in real-time. The audio description can be accessed through a smartphone app, allowing people with visual disabilities to access audio descriptions in any situation.

Another example of an AI-powered audio description system is the Microsoft Seeing AI app. The app uses computer vision and machine learning algorithms to provide audio descriptions for people with visual disabilities. The app can recognize objects, people, and text in the user's environment and provide a verbal description of them. The app can also recognize handwriting and read aloud written text, allowing people with visual disabilities to access written content.

AI-powered audio description systems can also improve the accuracy and consistency of audio descriptions. Traditional audio description methods can be subjective and may vary depending on the person providing the description. In contrast, AI-powered audio description systems use machine learning algorithms that are trained on large datasets of audio descriptions. This can help to ensure that audio descriptions are accurate, consistent, and of high quality.

AI-powered audio description systems can also reduce the cost of producing audio descriptions. Traditional audio description methods require specialized audio recording equipment, trained audio describers, and post-production editing. This can be time-consuming and expensive. In contrast, AI-powered audio description systems can generate audio descriptions in real-time using computer vision and natural language processing technologies. This can help to reduce the cost of producing audio descriptions and make them more widely available.

In addition to providing real-time audio descriptions, AI-powered systems can also improve the accessibility of live events. Live events, such as theater performances and sports events, can be challenging for people with visual disabilities to access because they may not have access to audio descriptions in real-time. AI-powered audio description systems can help to address this issue by providing real-time audio descriptions of live events. The system can use computer vision algorithms to analyze the visual content and generate real-time audio descriptions of the event.

Overall, AI-powered audio description systems have the potential to significantly enhance the accessibility of visual content for people with visual disabilities. These systems can provide real-time audio descriptions that are accurate, consistent, and of high quality. They can also reduce the cost of producing audio descriptions and make them more widely available. As such, AI-powered audio description systems represent a significant step forward in enhancing the accessibility of visual content for people with visual disabilities.

AI in Accessibility Planning and Design

In addition to providing accessibility services, AI can also be used in accessibility planning and design. AI-powered systems can help to identify accessibility barriers and suggest solutions to improve accessibility for people with disabilities.

One example of an AI-powered accessibility planning system is the CitySwipe app. CitySwipe uses machine learning algorithms to collect feedback from citizens with disabilities about accessibility barriers in their communities. The app then uses this feedback to suggest improvements to public spaces, transportation systems, and other areas that may pose accessibility challenges.

Another example of an AI-powered accessibility design system is the Google Maps Accessible Places feature. The feature uses machine learning to identify and highlight accessible places on Google Maps, such as wheelchair-friendly entrances, parking spaces, and restrooms. This can help people with disabilities navigate their communities more easily and independently.

AI can also be used to enhance accessibility in public transportation. For example, the Singapore Land Transport Authority has developed an AI-powered system called Beeline that helps people with disabilities plan their transit routes. The system uses machine learning algorithms to analyze real-time data on bus and train schedules, as well as accessibility features such as wheelchair ramps and priority seating, to provide personalized transit recommendations for people with disabilities.

In addition to improving accessibility in physical spaces and transportation, AI can also enhance accessibility in digital environments. For example, the Microsoft Seeing AI app uses machine learning algorithms to provide real-time audio descriptions of a user's surroundings, such as people, objects, and text. The app can also recognize and read aloud text on signs and documents, making it easier for people with visual impairments to navigate and access information.

Another example of AI-powered accessibility in digital environments is the use of real-time captioning. AI-powered captioning systems, such as Google's Live Caption feature, use machine learning algorithms to transcribe spoken words into text in real-time. This can help people with hearing impairments follow conversations, lectures, and other spoken content in real-time.

AI can also be used to enhance accessibility in communication. For example, the Ava app uses machine learning algorithms to provide real-time captioning for group conversations, making it easier for people with hearing impairments to participate in conversations with multiple speakers. The app can also identify and differentiate between different speakers, making it easier for users to follow along with who is speaking.

Finally, AI can be used to enhance accessibility in emergency situations. For example, the California Governor's Office of Emergency Services has developed an AI-powered system called Accessible Hazard Alert System (AHAS) that provides real-time emergency alerts in multiple formats, including text-to-speech, captioning, and braille. This can help ensure that people with disabilities receive critical emergency information in a timely and accessible manner.

AI has the potential to significantly enhance accessibility for people with disabilities in various aspects of daily life, including physical spaces, transportation, digital environments, communication, and emergency situations. AI-powered systems for sign language interpretation, real-time captioning, and audio descriptions can help make information and communication more accessible, while AI-powered accessibility planning and design systems can help ensure that physical spaces and transportation are designed with accessibility in mind. As AI continues to develop, it is important that local governments and communities continue to explore and invest in the potential of AI to enhance accessibility and inclusivity for all citizens.

Chapter 14: Improving Financial Management with AI

Financial management is a crucial function of local government, as it involves planning, organizing, directing, and controlling financial resources to achieve organizational goals and objectives. However, managing financial resources can be complex and time-consuming, especially in the face of changing economic conditions and evolving regulatory requirements. Fortunately, advancements in artificial intelligence (AI) have opened new possibilities for financial management in local government. AI-powered systems can help improve financial forecasting and analysis, detect, and prevent fraud, and enhance revenue management. In this chapter, we will explore the use of AI in financial management and its benefits for local government.

AI-powered systems for budget forecasting and analysis

One of the most promising applications of AI in financial management is the use of AI-powered systems for budget forecasting and analysis. Budget forecasting and analysis are essential for local governments as they enable them to plan and allocate resources effectively, ensure fiscal stability, and meet their financial obligations.

AI-powered systems for budget forecasting and analysis use machine learning algorithms to analyze historical financial data, economic indicators, and other relevant information to forecast future revenues and expenses. By leveraging vast amounts of data, these systems can help local governments make more accurate budget decisions and adjust spending plans as needed.

One example of an AI-powered system for budget forecasting and analysis is the Budget Maestro platform. Budget Maestro is a financial planning and analysis software that uses machine learning algorithms to analyze historical financial data and identify trends and patterns that can be used to forecast future revenues and expenses. The platform can also simulate various budget scenarios and provide recommendations for budget adjustments based on projected revenue and expense trends.

Budget Maestro enables local governments to create accurate and reliable budgets by providing them with a comprehensive view of their financial performance. The platform can also help local governments to identify potential risks and opportunities, allowing them to make informed decisions about future investments and spending.

Another example of an AI-powered system for budget forecasting and analysis is the Anaplan platform. Anaplan is a cloud-based financial planning and analysis software that uses machine learning algorithms to analyze financial data and provide real-time budget forecasts and scenarios. The platform can integrate with other financial management systems to provide a comprehensive view of the organization's financial performance.

One example of an AI-powered system for revenue management is the IDeaS Revenue Management System. This platform uses machine learning algorithms to analyze data from various sources, such as historical booking data, market demand, and competitor pricing, to optimize pricing and revenue strategies. The system can also provide real-time alerts and recommendations for pricing adjustments based on changes in market conditions.

Another example of an AI-powered revenue management system is the Rainmaker platform. Rainmaker uses machine learning algorithms to analyze data from multiple sources, such as historical booking data, website traffic, and market demand, to provide real-time pricing recommendations. The platform can also simulate various pricing scenarios and provide recommendations for revenue optimization based on projected demand.

AI-powered revenue management systems can help local governments increase revenue and profitability while minimizing the risk of revenue loss due to inaccurate pricing decisions. These systems can also help local governments stay competitive by providing real-time insights into market conditions and competitor pricing.

Anaplan enables local governments to create more accurate budgets by providing them with real-time financial data and insights. The platform can also help local governments to collaborate on budget planning and analysis, allowing multiple stakeholders to contribute to the budgeting process.

In addition to budget forecasting and analysis, AI can also be used in financial management to detect and prevent fraud. Fraud detection is an essential function of financial management, as it helps to protect local governments from financial losses and reputational damage.

AI-powered systems for fraud detection use machine learning algorithms to analyze financial data and identify anomalies and suspicious transactions. By identifying potential fraud early on, these systems can help local governments to take corrective action and prevent further losses.

One example of an AI-powered system for fraud detection is the FraudLens platform. FraudLens uses machine learning algorithms to analyze financial data and identify anomalies and suspicious transactions. The platform can also provide real-time alerts and notifications to help local governments respond to potential fraud quickly and effectively.

Another example of an AI-powered system for fraud detection is the Oracle Financial Crime and Compliance Management platform. Oracle Financial Crime and Compliance Management uses machine learning algorithms to analyze financial data and identify suspicious transactions. The platform can also integrate with other financial management systems to provide a comprehensive view of the organization's financial performance.

AI-powered systems for fraud detection can help local governments to protect themselves from financial losses and reputational damage. By identifying potential fraud early on, these systems can enable local governments to take corrective action and prevent further losses.

In addition to budget forecasting, analysis, and fraud detection, AI can also be used in financial management for revenue management. Revenue management is the process of optimizing pricing and inventory to maximize revenue.

AI-powered systems for revenue management use machine learning algorithms to analyze customer behavior, market trends, and other relevant information to optimize pricing and inventory. By leveraging vast amounts of data, these systems can help local governments to maximize revenue and improve financial performance.

Fraud detection

AI-powered systems have proven to be highly effective in detecting and preventing fraudulent activity in local government financial management. These systems use machine learning algorithms to analyze large amounts of financial data and detect anomalies and patterns that may indicate fraudulent activity. By doing so, they can help local governments save millions of dollars that would otherwise be lost to fraud.

One of the most popular AI-powered systems for fraud detection is the MindBridge Ai Auditor platform. This platform uses machine learning algorithms to analyze financial data and identify anomalies and patterns that may indicate fraudulent activity. The platform is highly versatile and can be used to detect a wide range of fraudulent activity, such as embezzlement, theft, and misuse of public funds.

One of the key advantages of the MindBridge Ai Auditor platform is its ability to analyze large volumes of financial data quickly and accurately. The platform can detect patterns and anomalies that would be difficult, if not impossible, for humans to identify. This allows local governments to detect fraudulent activity more quickly and accurately than they would be able to otherwise.

The MindBridge Ai Auditor platform also provides recommendations for how to address suspected fraudulent activity. This helps local governments take swift and appropriate action to prevent further fraudulent activity and minimize financial losses. The platform can also be customized to meet the specific needs of local governments, ensuring that it provides the most effective fraud detection and prevention solutions possible.

Another popular AI-powered system for fraud detection is the Verafin platform. Verafin uses machine learning algorithms to analyze financial data and detect suspicious activity, such as unusual transactions or behavior patterns. The platform can also integrate with other financial management systems to provide a comprehensive view of the organization's financial performance and detect potential fraud.

The Verafin platform is highly effective at detecting fraudulent activity and has been used successfully by many local governments. It is also highly customizable, allowing local governments to tailor the platform to their specific needs and requirements. This ensures that the platform provides the most effective fraud detection and prevention solutions possible.

Revenue management

AI has the potential to revolutionize financial management in local government by improving efficiency, reducing costs, and enhancing accuracy. One of the most promising applications of AI in financial management is its use in budget forecasting and analysis. AI-powered systems can analyze historical financial data, economic indicators, and other relevant information to forecast future revenues and expenses. This can help local governments make more accurate budget decisions and adjust spending plans as needed.

For instance, the Budget Maestro platform uses machine learning algorithms to analyze historical financial data and identify trends and patterns that can be used to forecast future revenues and expenses. It can also simulate various budget scenarios and provide recommendations for budget adjustments based on projected revenue and expense trends. Another example of an AI-powered system for budget forecasting and analysis is the Anaplan platform, which uses machine learning algorithms to analyze financial data and provide real-time budget forecasts and scenarios. The platform can integrate with other financial management systems to provide a comprehensive view of the organization's financial performance.

AI can also enhance financial management in local government by improving revenue management. AI-powered systems can analyze financial data and identify opportunities for revenue growth, including identifying new sources of revenue, optimizing existing revenue streams, and reducing revenue leakage. The Cognos Analytics platform, for instance, uses machine learning algorithms to analyze financial data and identify opportunities for revenue growth. It can also provide recommendations for how to optimize revenue streams and reduce revenue leakage, enabling local governments to maximize their revenue potential. Similarly, the Oracle Revenue Management Cloud platform uses machine learning algorithms to analyze financial data and identify revenue opportunities. It can integrate with other financial management systems to provide a comprehensive view of the organization's financial performance and revenue potential.

Moreover, AI can also be utilized for fraud detection, which is a crucial aspect of financial management in local government. Fraud can occur in many forms, such as embezzlement, theft, and misuse of public funds. AI-powered systems can help detect and prevent fraud by analyzing financial data for anomalies and patterns that may indicate fraudulent activity. The MindBridge Ai Auditor platform, for instance, uses machine learning algorithms to analyze financial data and identify anomalies and patterns that may indicate fraudulent activity. It can also provide recommendations for how to address suspected fraudulent activity, enabling local governments to take swift and appropriate action. Similarly, the Verafin platform uses machine learning algorithms to analyze financial data and detect suspicious activity, such as unusual transactions or behavior patterns. It can integrate with other financial management systems to provide a comprehensive view of the organization's financial performance and detect potential fraud.

Additionally, AI can also improve financial management in local government by automating routine financial management tasks, such as accounts payable and accounts receivable. This can help reduce errors, improve efficiency, and reduce costs. The Xero platform, for instance, uses machine learning algorithms to automate accounts payable and accounts receivable tasks. It can also provide real-time insights into the organization's financial performance, enabling local governments to make more informed decisions.

Another application of AI in financial management is its use in risk management. AI-powered systems can analyze financial data and identify potential risks, such as market fluctuations, fraud, and non-compliance with regulations. This can help local governments take proactive measures to mitigate these risks and protect their financial assets. The IBM Watson platform, for instance, uses machine learning algorithms to analyze financial data and identify potential risks. It can also provide recommendations for how to mitigate these risks, enabling local governments to take proactive measures to protect their financial assets.

Furthermore, AI can also be utilized for tax compliance and reporting. AI-powered systems can analyze financial data and ensure that local governments comply with relevant tax laws and regulations. The Taxo.ai[1] platform, for instance, uses machine learning algorithms to analyze financial data and ensure tax compliance. It can also generate

---

1.   http://taxo.ai/

tax reports and provide recommendations for how to optimize tax strategies, enabling to better align with legal, regulatory, and/or contractual requirements.

There are several examples of local government organizations that have implemented AI for financial management after 2021. One such example is the city of New York, which has been using AI-powered tools to improve its budget forecasting and analysis. In 2021, the city launched an AI-based forecasting tool to provide more accurate and timely revenue projections, enabling better financial planning and management.

Another example is the city of Las Vegas, which has been using AI-powered systems to improve revenue management. In 2021, the city implemented an AI-based revenue optimization tool that uses machine learning algorithms to analyze data and identify opportunities for revenue growth. The tool has helped the city identify new revenue streams and optimize existing ones, resulting in increased revenue and reduced costs.

In addition to budget forecasting, revenue management, and risk management, AI has also been used in local governments for fraud detection. For example, the city of San Diego has implemented an AI-powered system for fraud detection in its tax collection process. The system uses machine learning algorithms to analyze financial data and detect anomalies and patterns that may indicate fraudulent activity, enabling the city to take appropriate action to prevent and address fraud.

Benefits of AI-powered financial management

The benefits of AI-powered financial management in local government are numerous. First and foremost, AI-powered systems can improve the accuracy and reliability of financial data, enabling local governments to make more informed decisions. AI can also help reduce the time and effort required to perform financial management tasks, freeing up staff to focus on other important areas. Additionally, AI-powered systems can help reduce the risk of fraud and other financial irregularities by quickly detecting anomalies and suspicious patterns in financial data.

Another benefit of AI-powered financial management is increased efficiency. AI can automate many financial management tasks, such as data entry and analysis, budget forecasting, and report generation. This can save local governments significant amounts of time and money, as staff can focus on more complex tasks that require human judgment and decision-making.

AI-powered financial management can also help local governments optimize their revenue streams. For example, AI-powered revenue management systems can analyze data from various sources, such as sales data, customer demographics, and market trends, to identify opportunities for increasing revenue. These systems can also generate personalized pricing strategies and targeted marketing campaigns to maximize revenue.

Despite the many benefits of AI-powered financial management, there are also some potential drawbacks and challenges. One of the main challenges is the need for high-quality data. AI-powered systems rely on accurate and comprehensive data to make accurate predictions and recommendations. Therefore, local governments need to invest in data management and quality control processes to ensure that their financial data is reliable and up to date.

Another challenge is the need for skilled staff who can develop, implement, and maintain AI-powered financial management systems. Local governments need to invest in training and development programs to ensure that their staff has the necessary skills and knowledge to work with AI-powered systems.

Additionally, there are ethical and privacy concerns associated with the use of AI in financial management. For example, AI-powered systems may be biased or unfair if they are trained on data that reflects historical biases or discrimination. Local governments need to develop ethical frameworks and guidelines for the use of AI in financial management to ensure that these systems are transparent, fair, and unbiased.

Overall, the benefits of AI-powered financial management in local government are significant. AI can help local governments make more informed decisions, increase efficiency, and optimize revenue streams. However, there are also challenges and potential risks associated with the use of AI in financial management. Local governments need to invest in data management and quality control processes, as well as training and development programs for staff. They also need to develop ethical frameworks and guidelines to ensure that AI-powered systems are transparent, fair, and unbiased.

Chapter 15: Improving Human Resources with AI

Human resources (HR) are a critical function in any organization, responsible for managing employee needs, recruitment, training, and retention. In recent years, artificial intelligence (AI) has emerged as a tool to enhance the capabilities of HR professionals and improve the overall efficiency of HR processes. AI can automate tedious tasks, identify the best candidates for open positions, predict employee turnover, and improve the overall employee experience. This chapter will explore the various ways in which AI is transforming HR and the potential benefits and risks associated with its use.

Recruitment and Onboarding

One of the most promising applications of AI in the field of human resources is in recruitment and onboarding. Traditional recruitment and onboarding processes can be time-consuming and tedious for both HR professionals and job candidates. The process of sifting through resumes, screening candidates, and conducting interviews is not only time-consuming but also prone to human error. AI-powered systems have the potential to streamline these processes, reduce the workload of HR professionals, and improve the quality of hires.

Recruitment is a crucial aspect of human resource management as it is essential to find the right candidate for the job. AI-powered systems can help HR professionals identify the best candidates for open positions by analyzing resumes, job descriptions, and other relevant data. These systems can also automate the initial screening process, reducing the workload of HR professionals. An example of such a system is the HireVue platform. HireVue uses machine learning algorithms to analyze video interviews and identify the best candidates for open positions. The platform can also analyze facial expressions and other non-verbal cues to assess a candidate's fit for a particular role.

The HireVue platform has been adopted by companies such as Unilever and Goldman Sachs to automate their recruitment processes. The platform allows candidates to record their answers to pre-set questions through their webcam or mobile device, which are then analyzed by the AI algorithms. The algorithms analyze various factors such as tone, facial expressions, body language, and word choice to evaluate the candidate's responses. The system can also assess a candidate's cultural fit with the company based on their responses to certain questions. This technology has the potential to level the playing field for job candidates, reducing the impact of unconscious biases that may affect the hiring process.

Another example of an AI-powered system for recruitment is the Mya chatbot. The chatbot can engage with candidates via text message, email, or chat, asking questions and providing information about the job and the hiring process. Mya can also screen resumes and schedule interviews, reducing the workload of HR professionals. The chatbot uses natural language processing (NLP) to understand and respond to candidate queries, providing a personalized and efficient experience for job candidates.

Onboarding is another area where AI can be used to enhance the employee experience. Onboarding refers to the process of integrating new employees into an organization and providing them with the information and tools they need to be productive. This process can be time-consuming and tedious for both HR professionals and new hires. AI-powered chatbots can answer common questions and provide information to new hires, reducing the workload of HR professionals and ensuring a smooth onboarding process.

For example, the chatbot from One Model can help new hires navigate the onboarding process by answering common questions, such as where to find HR policies or how to enroll in benefits. The chatbot can also provide personalized information to new hires based on their role, location, and other factors. This personalized onboarding experience can help new hires feel more welcome and engaged with the organization, increasing their likelihood of staying with the company.

AI-powered systems can also help HR professionals identify and address issues that may arise during the onboarding process. For example, the Talla chatbot can monitor employee feedback during onboarding and alert HR professionals to any issues or concerns that arise. This proactive approach can help HR professionals address issues before they become major problems, reducing turnover and improving employee engagement.

Employee Experience

Employee experience has become an increasingly important focus for organizations in recent years, as companies recognize the link between employee satisfaction and productivity. One way that organizations are seeking to enhance the employee experience is by incorporating AI-powered solutions into their HR practices.

AI can be used to provide personalized learning and development opportunities for employees, which can help to improve their job satisfaction and performance. By analyzing employee data, AI-powered systems can identify areas where employees may need additional training or support and provide personalized recommendations to help employees reach their career goals. For example, the IBM Watson Career Coach platform uses machine learning algorithms to analyze employee data and provide personalized recommendations for learning and development.

Another way that AI can be used to enhance the employee experience is by identifying potential sources of employee dissatisfaction. By analyzing employee data, AI-powered systems can identify patterns or trends that may be contributing to employee turnover or low job satisfaction. This information can then be used by HR professionals to make targeted improvements to the work environment or company culture. For example, an AI-powered system could identify that employees who work in open office environments are more likely to report low job satisfaction, which could lead HR to implement changes to the office layout or provide more opportunities for private workspaces.

AI can also facilitate employee feedback, which is a critical component of a positive employee experience. By using AI-powered systems to collect feedback from employees, organizations can ensure that they are receiving honest and actionable feedback, which can be used to improve the employee experience. For example, an AI-powered chatbot could be used to collect anonymous feedback from employees on a regular basis, allowing employees to provide feedback on their experiences without fear of retaliation or negative consequences.

One example of an AI-powered system for employee feedback is the Glint platform. Glint uses natural language processing and machine learning algorithms to analyze employee feedback and identify patterns or trends in employee sentiment. The platform can also provide HR professionals with recommendations for improving the employee experience based on this feedback.

In addition to providing personalized learning and development opportunities, identifying potential sources of employee dissatisfaction, and facilitating employee feedback, AI can also be used to enhance other aspects of the employee experience, such as onboarding and employee engagement.

AI-powered chatbots can be used to provide personalized onboarding experiences for new hires, answering common questions and providing information about company policies and procedures. This can help to ensure that new hires feel welcomed and supported as they transition into their new roles.

Employee engagement is another critical component of a positive employee experience, and AI can be used to enhance engagement by providing personalized recommendations for employee recognition and rewards. By analyzing employee data, AI-powered systems can identify high-performing employees and provide recommendations for rewards or recognition that are tailored to each employee's individual preferences and motivations.

One example of an AI-powered system for employee recognition and rewards is the Bonusly platform. Bonusly uses machine learning algorithms to analyze employee data and provide personalized recommendations for rewards and recognition. The platform allows employees to give and receive recognition from their peers, which can help to foster a culture of appreciation and recognition within the organization.

Process Improvement

Human resources (HR) departments are responsible for a variety of functions that impact the overall success of an organization, from recruiting and onboarding new employees to managing performance and facilitating employee development. The implementation of artificial intelligence (AI) in HR has the potential to enhance these processes by improving accuracy, reducing bias, and increasing efficiency. AI can help HR professionals identify the best candidates for open positions, automate routine tasks, and provide personalized recommendations for employee development. In this paper, we will discuss how AI can improve HR processes and provide examples of AI-powered systems currently in use.

Automating HR Tasks

One of the most significant advantages of AI in HR is the ability to automate routine tasks such as data entry and analysis. By automating these tasks, HR professionals can focus on more strategic responsibilities such as talent development and employee engagement.

AI-powered systems can also reduce the risk of human error and provide faster and more accurate results. Examples of tasks that can be automated with AI include:

- Resume screening: AI can analyze resumes and job descriptions to identify the best candidates for open positions. This can save HR professionals a significant amount of time and reduce the risk of bias in the recruiting process.
- Performance reviews: AI can automate the performance review process by providing a structured framework for evaluations and identifying areas for improvement. This can help ensure that all employees receive consistent and fair feedback.
- Employee data analysis: AI can analyze employee data such as attendance and performance metrics to identify trends and potential sources of inefficiency. This can help HR professionals make data-driven decisions about talent development and process improvement.

AI-Powered Systems for Process Improvement

In addition to automating routine tasks, AI can also be used to identify potential sources of inefficiency in HR processes and provide recommendations for improvement. This can help organizations optimize their HR processes and improve overall efficiency. Examples of AI-powered systems for process improvement include:

- SAP SuccessFactors: SAP SuccessFactors uses machine learning algorithms to automate HR tasks such as performance reviews and employee data analysis. The platform can also provide recommendations for process improvements based on the analysis of HR data.

- Workday: Workday uses AI to identify potential sources of inefficiency in HR processes and provide recommendations for improvement. The platform can also automate routine HR tasks such as data entry and provide real-time insights into workforce trends.
- ADP DataCloud: ADP DataCloud uses AI to analyze HR data and identify potential sources of inefficiency in the recruiting and hiring process. The platform can also provide insights into workforce demographics and trends.

AI-Powered Systems for Recruitment and Onboarding

One of the most promising applications of AI in HR is in recruitment and onboarding. AI-powered systems can help HR professionals identify the best candidates for open positions by analyzing resumes, job descriptions, and other relevant data. These systems can also automate the initial screening process, reducing the workload of HR professionals. Examples of AI-powered systems for recruitment and onboarding include:

- HireVue: HireVue uses machine learning algorithms to analyze video interviews and identify the best candidates for open positions. The platform can also analyze facial expressions and other non-verbal cues to assess a candidate's fit for a particular role.
- Entelo: Entelo uses AI to analyze candidate data and identify the best candidates for open positions. The platform can also provide insights into candidate demographics and trends.
- Textio: Textio uses AI to analyze job descriptions and identify potential sources of bias. The platform can also provide recommendations for more inclusive language and help organizations attract a more diverse pool of candidates.

AI-Powered Systems for Employee Experience

The employee experience is a crucial aspect of any organization's success, as it can greatly impact employee engagement, satisfaction, and retention. In recent years, there has been a growing trend towards using AI to enhance the employee experience, particularly in learning and development.

One of the keyways that AI can be used to enhance the employee experience is by providing personalized learning and development opportunities. Traditional learning and development programs often use a one-size-fits-all approach, which can be ineffective for employees with different learning styles and preferences. AI-powered learning platforms, on the other hand, can provide customized learning experiences that are tailored to each employee's individual needs.

An example of an AI-powered learning platform is EdApp, which uses machine learning algorithms to create personalized training modules for employees based on their job roles, learning preferences, and performance data. The platform can also provide real-time feedback and assessments to help employees improve their skills and knowledge.

Another example of an AI-powered platform for learning and development is Degreed. Degreed uses AI to curate personalized learning experiences for employees based on their interests, skills, and career goals. The platform can also track employees' progress and provide recommendations for further learning opportunities.

By providing personalized learning and development opportunities, AI can help employees feel more engaged and valued, which can lead to improved job satisfaction and retention. Additionally, by improving employees' skills and knowledge, organizations can enhance their overall performance and competitiveness in the marketplace.

However, it's important to note that AI is not a silver bullet solution for learning and development. It's important to ensure that

AI-powered learning platforms are designed with a human-centered approach that considers employees' individual needs and preferences. Additionally, organizations must ensure that AI-powered learning platforms are transparent and accountable, and that employees can provide feedback and input into the learning process.

Risk Management

AI can play a significant role in managing HR-related risks, such as employee turnover and compliance with regulations. By analyzing HR data, AI-powered systems can identify potential sources of risk and provide recommendations for mitigating these risks, enabling HR professionals to take proactive measures to protect their organization.

One example of an AI-powered system for risk management is the Workday platform. Workday is a cloud-based HR management system that uses machine learning algorithms to analyze HR data and provide actionable insights to HR professionals. The platform can identify potential sources of risk, such as high employee turnover rates or non-compliance with regulations and provide recommendations for mitigating these risks.

One way in which AI can help manage HR-related risks is by identifying potential sources of employee turnover. High employee turnover rates can be costly for organizations, both in terms of lost productivity and the time and resources required to hire and train new employees. By analyzing HR data such as employee satisfaction surveys, performance reviews, and exit interviews, AI-powered systems can identify factors that may be contributing to high turnover rates, such as low employee engagement or inadequate training opportunities. HR professionals can then take proactive steps to address these issues, such as implementing new training programs or improving employee engagement initiatives.

AI can also help organizations stay compliant with regulations. HR regulations can be complex and ever-changing, making it challenging for HR professionals to keep up with the latest requirements. AI-powered systems can analyze HR data to ensure that organizations are complying with relevant regulations, such as those related to equal employment opportunity or employee benefits. For example, AI can help ensure that job postings are compliant with regulations, such as using gender-neutral language, and that employee benefit packages meet legal requirements.

Another way in which AI can help manage HR-related risks is by identifying potential sources of workplace accidents and injuries. Workplace accidents and injuries can be costly for organizations, both in terms of the financial costs of worker's compensation claims and the negative impact on employee morale. By analyzing HR data such as safety records and employee health data, AI-powered systems can identify potential safety risks and provide recommendations for mitigating these risks. For example, AI can help identify employees who are at higher risk of injury based on their job duties and provide recommendations for how to reduce these risks, such as implementing new safety procedures or providing additional training.

AI can also help organizations manage risks related to employee misconduct. Employee misconduct, such as harassment or discrimination, can have serious consequences for organizations, including legal liability and damage to their reputation. By analyzing HR data such as employee complaints and disciplinary records, AI-powered systems can identify potential sources of misconduct and provide recommendations for mitigating these risks. For example, AI can help identify employees who may be at higher risk of engaging in misconduct based on their job duties or past behavior and provide recommendations for how to reduce these risks, such as implementing new training programs or conducting more frequent performance reviews.

Challenges and Risks

While AI has the potential to transform HR, there are also challenges and risks associated with its use. One major challenge is the need for high-quality data. AI-powered systems rely on data to make decisions, so it is essential that HR professionals ensure the data they are using is accurate and relevant.

One of the challenges of using AI-powered systems in HR processes is the potential for bias to be perpetuated, particularly if the data used to train the AI is biased itself. However, it is important to note that bias in AI systems can stem not only from biased data, but also from human biases and systemic, institutional biases.

Some common types of bias that can be perpetuated by AI systems include sampling bias, which occurs when the data used to train the system is not representative of the population being analyzed, and cognitive biases, which are unconscious errors in thinking that can affect individuals' judgments and decisions. Additionally, conscious, and unconscious biases can creep into the recruiting process, resulting in the rejection of deserving candidates.

To mitigate the potential for bias in AI-powered HR systems, it is important to identify potential sources of bias and develop strategies to mitigate them. This can involve careful data selection and analysis, as well as ongoing monitoring of the AI system to ensure that it is making fair and unbiased decisions. It is also important to recognize that AI systems can only be as objective as the data they are built on, and that historical data may reflect societal biases at the time it was generated.

Overall, the potential for bias is an important consideration when implementing AI-powered HR systems, and steps must be taken to ensure that these systems are making fair and unbiased decisions. By carefully selecting and analyzing data, monitoring the system for bias, and recognizing the potential for cognitive and unconscious biases to creep into the recruiting process, HR professionals can leverage the benefits of AI while minimizing the potential for bias to be perpetuated.

Chapter 17: The future of Artificial Intelligence with Information Technology

Artificial intelligence (AI) has made significant strides over the past decade, and its impact on the field of information technology (IT) has been profound. In Chapter 17, we explore the future of AI and IT, including the potential applications of AI in IT, the challenges and ethical considerations surrounding its development and implementation, and the potential impact on the workforce and society.

AI has already made significant contributions to the field of IT, from improving cybersecurity to streamlining business processes. However, the potential applications of AI in IT go far beyond what we have seen so far.

Cybersecurity

Artificial Intelligence (AI) has transformed numerous industries, and one of the most significant areas of impact has been cybersecurity. With the increasing dependence on digital networks and the rise of cyber threats, the need for robust and efficient security measures has never been more critical. AI-powered systems have demonstrated their potential in identifying and responding to threats in real-time, thereby aiding organizations in preventing cyber-attacks and data breaches. As we look forward, we can anticipate AI to further enhance the accuracy and efficiency of threat detection and automate incident response, thereby revolutionizing the cybersecurity landscape.

Threat Detection

AI algorithms, particularly machine learning and deep learning techniques, have significantly improved threat detection. By processing large amounts of data and identifying patterns, AI systems can detect known threats and identify new, unknown threats more accurately than traditional rule-based systems.

Darktrace, a leading cybersecurity firm, uses AI to detect and respond to threats in real-time. Their system learns the normal patterns of behavior within a network and detects any anomalies that could indicate a potential cyber-attack.

Phishing Detection

Phishing attacks, where attackers attempt to steal sensitive information by masquerading as a trustworthy entity, are common and can have severe consequences. AI systems can analyze emails, text messages, and other forms of communication to detect phishing attempts based on the content, patterns, and other factors.

An example is Google's Gmail uses machine learning algorithms to identify and block phishing emails. The system assesses factors such as sender reputation, email content, and past user interactions to determine if an email is a phishing attempt.

Vulnerability Management

AI can help organizations identify and prioritize vulnerabilities in their systems, making it easier to address potential threats. Machine learning algorithms can analyze vast amounts of data to detect vulnerabilities, understand the risks they pose, and suggest appropriate remediation steps.

Kenna Security's platform uses AI to help organizations prioritize vulnerabilities based on real-world exploitability and the potential impact of a breach, allowing for more efficient remediation efforts.

Future Applications of AI in Cybersecurity

Enhanced Threat Prediction

As AI algorithms continue to improve, we can expect even more accurate threat prediction capabilities. Advanced AI systems will be able to identify new attack vectors, forecast potential cyber-attacks, and provide proactive security measures to prevent breaches before they occur.

Cybereason, a cybersecurity company, is working on an AI-driven platform that can predict and prevent cyber-attacks. The platform will use advanced machine learning algorithms to understand attacker behavior and identify emerging threats in real-time.

Automated Incident Response

Automation will play a crucial role in the future of cybersecurity, particularly in incident response. AI systems will be able to analyze security incidents, determine the most effective response, and execute remediation actions autonomously, reducing the time and resources required to address threats.

IBM's Resilient Incident Response Platform integrates AI capabilities to automate and orchestrate incident response processes, enabling organizations to respond to security incidents more efficiently and effectively.

AI-driven Security Awareness Training

AI can help design more effective security awareness training programs by identifying areas where employees are most likely to make mistakes or fall victim to cyber-attacks. By analyzing user behavior and tailoring training to address specific weaknesses, organizations can improve their overall security posture.

Companies like KnowBe4 and Elevate Security uses AI to analyze employee behavior and identify patterns that may indicate a higher risk of falling for a cyber-attack. The platform then provides targeted training and personalized recommendations to help employees improve their security awareness.

Data Analysis

Another area where AI has significant potential in IT is data analysis. AI-powered systems can analyze large datasets quickly and accurately, enabling organizations to gain insights that would be impossible to obtain using traditional methods. This can help organizations to make better-informed decisions, from product development to marketing and advertising.

Business Process Automation

AI can also be used to automate routine business processes, freeing up employees to focus on more complex tasks. This can include everything from automating customer service interactions to streamlining the procurement process. As AI technology improves, we can expect to see more and more business processes automated, leading to greater efficiency and cost savings.

The Challenges and Ethical Considerations Surrounding AI in IT

While the potential benefits of AI in IT are vast, there are also significant challenges and ethical considerations that must be addressed. In this section, we explore some of the key challenges and ethical considerations surrounding the development and implementation of AI in IT.

Bias

One of the most significant challenges surrounding the development and implementation of AI in IT is the potential for bias. AI-powered systems rely on data to make decisions, and if that data is biased, it can result in discriminatory outcomes. In this comprehensive overview, we will explore the issue of bias in AI, its causes, consequences, and potential solutions to ensure fair and unbiased AI systems.

Causes of Bias in AI

1. Biased Training Data

AI systems learn from the data they are trained on. If the training data contains biases or inaccuracies, the AI system is likely to adopt those biases in its decision-making. This is particularly true for machine learning algorithms, which learn patterns and associations from the data without explicit instructions. Biased training data can result from historical biases, sampling biases, or measurement errors.

1. Algorithmic Bias

Algorithmic bias occurs when the algorithms used in AI systems are inherently biased. This can happen when the algorithms are designed with certain assumptions or simplifications that lead to biased outcomes. In some cases, the algorithm may unintentionally magnify existing biases in the data, leading to even more biased results.

1. Lack of Diversity in Development Teams

The development of AI systems is influenced by the perspectives of those who create them. A lack of diversity among AI developers can lead to unconscious biases being built into the systems. This can result in AI systems that are more likely to have biased outcomes or be less effective for certain populations.

Consequences of Bias in AI

1. Discrimination

Biased AI systems can lead to discrimination in various sectors, including hiring, lending, healthcare, and law enforcement. For example, if an AI-powered recruitment system is trained on biased data that favors a certain gender, it may perpetuate that bias by recommending candidates of that gender over others.

1. Loss of Trust

When AI systems produce biased results, it undermines public trust in the technology. This can slow down the adoption of AI and hinder its potential benefits in various industries.

1. Legal and Ethical Concerns

Biased AI systems can lead to legal and ethical concerns, as they may violate anti-discrimination laws and ethical principles. Organizations that deploy biased AI systems may face legal consequences, reputational damage, and loss of business opportunities.

Potential Solutions to Address Bias in AI

1. Diverse and Representative Data

To ensure AI systems make unbiased decisions, it is crucial to use diverse and representative training data. This involves collecting data from various sources and ensuring it accurately represents the target population. Data preprocessing techniques can also be employed to identify and mitigate biases present in the data.

1. Algorithmic Fairness

Developing algorithms that prioritize fairness and reduce bias is essential. Techniques like re-sampling, re-weighting, or adversarial training can be used to minimize algorithmic bias. Additionally, explainable AI can help to understand the decision-making process of AI systems and identify potential sources of bias.

1. Diverse Development Teams

Promoting diversity in AI development teams can help reduce the likelihood of unconscious biases being built into AI systems. By incorporating diverse perspectives, AI developers can create systems that are more inclusive and fairer.

1. Continuous Monitoring and Evaluation

Regularly monitoring and evaluating AI systems for potential biases is essential. By implementing performance metrics that specifically measure fairness and bias, organizations can identify and address any issues that arise during the AI system's deployment.

Addressing bias in AI is a significant challenge that requires ongoing attention and effort. By understanding the causes and consequences of bias and implementing strategies to mitigate it, we can develop AI systems that are fair, inclusive, and beneficial to all.

Privacy

Privacy is a major ethical concern that arises with the development and implementation of AI in the IT industry. AI-powered systems often require vast amounts of data to operate efficiently, which can raise concerns about how personal data is collected, stored, and used.

Organizations must prioritize transparency when it comes to data collection and usage. They must clearly communicate to customers and employees what data is being collected, how it is being used, and who has access to it. This transparency builds trust and allows individuals to make informed decisions about their personal information.

Furthermore, organizations must take adequate steps to protect the privacy of their customers and employees. This includes implementing strong data security measures, such as encryption and access controls, to prevent unauthorized access to personal data. Organizations must also establish clear policies and procedures for handling data breaches and must be prepared to respond quickly and effectively in the event of a security incident.

Ultimately, protecting privacy is not only an ethical obligation but also a legal requirement. Organizations must comply with various data privacy laws, such as the General Data Protection Regulation (GDPR) in Europe and the California Consumer Privacy Act (CCPA) in the United States. Failure to comply with these laws can result in significant financial penalties and damage to an organization's reputation. Therefore, organizations must prioritize privacy as an integral part of their AI development and implementation strategies.

Job Displacement

Artificial Intelligence (AI) is changing the way we live and work. AI-powered systems are becoming increasingly advanced and can perform tasks that were previously thought to be the sole domain of humans. However, as AI technology improves, it raises concerns about job displacement. While AI-powered systems can lead to greater efficiency and cost savings for organizations, they can also have a significant impact on the workforce, particularly in industries that are heavily reliant on routine tasks. In this section we will explore the development of AI-powered systems and the concerns about job displacement that it raises.

The Development of AI-Powered Systems

AI-powered systems have come a long way since the development of the first AI system in the 1950s. The field of AI has seen significant progress in recent years due to advancements in machine learning, deep learning, and natural language processing. These advancements have enabled AI systems to process large amounts of data and make complex decisions based on that data. AI systems are now capable of performing tasks such as image recognition, speech recognition, and natural language processing.

The use of AI-powered systems is becoming increasingly common in industries such as healthcare, finance, and manufacturing. In healthcare, AI-powered systems are being used to diagnose diseases and develop treatment plans. In finance, AI-powered systems are being used to detect fraud and improve risk management. In manufacturing, AI-powered systems are being used to optimize production processes and improve quality control.

The Impact of AI on the Workforce

The rise of Artificial Intelligence (AI) technology has led to a new era of automation and digital transformation. AI-powered systems have the potential to bring about greater efficiency, accuracy, and cost savings for organizations. However, the use of AI technology also has a significant impact on the workforce. It is likely to replace some jobs that are currently performed by humans. This section explores the impact of AI on the workforce, with a focus on industries that are heavily reliant on routine tasks. It also examines the potential consequences for workers and the wider economy.

The use of AI technology is likely to have a significant impact on the workforce. According to a report by the McKinsey Global Institute, up to 800 million jobs could be displaced by automation by 2030. The report estimates that up to one-third of the global workforce may need to switch to new occupations or acquire new skills by 2030 due to the impact of AI on the workforce. The impact of AI on the workforce is likely to be most significant in developing countries, where many workers are employed in low-skilled jobs that are susceptible to automation.

Industries that are Heavily Reliant on Routine Tasks

The impact of AI on the workforce is likely to be felt most strongly in industries that are heavily reliant on routine tasks. These include manufacturing, transportation, and logistics. In manufacturing, AI-powered systems can be used to automate tasks such as assembly, quality control, and packaging. In transportation and logistics, AI-powered systems can be used to optimize delivery routes, reduce fuel consumption, and improve supply chain management.

In the manufacturing sector, AI is already being used to automate tasks such as product assembly, quality control, and packaging. According to a report by the International Federation of Robotics, there were 381,000 industrial robots installed in the manufacturing industry in 2017. This represents an increase of 30% compared to 2016. The use of AI-powered robots in manufacturing is expected to continue to grow in the coming years, leading to job displacement for many workers.

In the transportation and logistics sector, AI-powered systems can be used to optimize delivery routes, reduce fuel consumption, and improve supply chain management. For example, UPS uses AI-powered algorithms to optimize delivery routes for its drivers. The system considers factors such as traffic, road closures, and weather conditions to ensure that drivers take the most efficient route. This has led to cost savings for the company, but it has also led to job displacement for some drivers.

Consequences for Workers

The impact of AI on the workforce is likely to be significant, and it will have consequences for workers. One potential consequence is job displacement. As AI-powered systems become more prevalent, many jobs that are currently performed by humans will be replaced by machines. This will lead to job losses for many workers, particularly those who are employed in industries that are heavily reliant on routine tasks.

Another consequence of AI on the workforce is the need for workers to acquire new skills. As jobs are displaced by automation, workers will need to develop new skills to remain employable. This may involve retraining or acquiring new qualifications. However, there is a risk that some workers may not be able to acquire the skills that are required to remain employable, leading to long-term unemployment.

The impact of AI on the workforce may also lead to changes in work. As routine tasks are automated, workers may be required to perform more complex and creative tasks. This may require workers to develop new skills and to adapt to new working practices. However, it may also lead to job satisfaction and improved working conditions for some workers.

The Impact of AI on Local Government

AI is expected to have a significant impact on local government over the next 10 years. According to Forbes, local governments are being called upon to be at the forefront of technology adoption, using AI to tackle challenges such as economic enablement during the pandemic. AI has the potential to enhance the effectiveness and efficiency of each stage of policymaking by giving decision-makers the tools to deliver more value to their constituents. AI and data analytics can help policymakers make sense of demographic, consumption, behavioral, and other trends in nearly all government sectors, helping them identify emerging issues and intervene with appropriate solutions.

AI is being implemented in various areas of local government to streamline processes and increase efficiency. One area where AI is being used is in asset maintenance systems. AI algorithms can analyze data from sensors and predict when maintenance will be required on critical infrastructure such as roads, bridges, and water systems. By predicting maintenance requirements, governments can reduce costs by avoiding unnecessary repairs and reducing downtime.

Another area where AI is being utilized in local government is in automated decision-making. AI algorithms can analyze large amounts of data and provide insights to help decision-makers identify the best course of action. For example, AI could be used to analyze traffic patterns and determine the best time to start road repairs to minimize traffic congestion. This could result in significant time and cost savings.

Machine learning and deep learning are also being used in local government to analyze data from various sources such as social media, news reports, and weather forecasts. This can help governments identify emerging issues and intervene with appropriate solutions before they become major problems. For example, during a natural disaster, AI algorithms can analyze social media data to identify areas where people are reporting problems such as blocked roads, power outages, or shortages of food and water. Governments can then use this information to allocate resources more effectively.

Natural language processing and neural networks are being used to improve citizen services. For example, AI-powered chatbots can be used to answer citizens' questions about government services and provide them with relevant information. This can reduce the burden on government staff and provide citizens with faster and more accurate responses.

Finally, robotic process automation is being used in local government to automate repetitive tasks such as data entry and document processing. This can free up staff time to focus on more complex and higher-value tasks, leading to greater efficiency and cost savings.

As AI continues to be implemented in local government, it is likely that many jobs will be impacted. While the exact number of jobs that will be eliminated is difficult to predict, studies show that AI is already having a significant impact on the workforce.

According to a 2022 survey by Deloitte, 56% of government leaders reported that they had already begun to automate tasks through AI. In addition, the McKinsey Global Institute estimates that by 2030, up to 375 million workers globally could be displaced by automation and AI.

Local government jobs that are at high risk of being impacted by AI include those that involve routine, repetitive tasks such as data entry, document processing, and customer service. These tasks can easily be automated by AI-powered tools such as chatbots and robotic process automation. In addition, some government jobs that involve decision-making and data analysis may also be impacted as AI can provide insights and recommendations to aid in decision-making.

It is important to note that while AI may lead to job displacement, it can also create new job opportunities. According to the same Deloitte survey, 77% of government leaders reported that AI has created new job roles in their organizations. These new jobs are typically focused on tasks that require skills such as data analysis, programming, and project management.

Governments can take steps to mitigate the impact of AI on the workforce. For example, they can invest in retraining and upskilling programs for workers whose jobs are at risk of being automated. This can help workers transition into new roles that require higher-level skills. Governments can also work with industry and education partners to ensure that workers are being trained for jobs that are in high demand.

While the implementation of AI in local government is expected to bring several benefits, it may also lead to the elimination of many jobs. However, governments can take steps to mitigate the impact on the workforce by investing in retraining and upskilling programs and ensuring that workers are being trained for jobs that are in high demand. By doing so, governments can ensure that their workforce is prepared for the jobs of the future.

The Response to Job Displacement due to AI

The potential impact of AI on the workforce has been a concern for many years, and in 2023, it continues to be a topic of discussion. As AI continues to be implemented in various industries, including local government, there are calls for action to mitigate the negative effects of job displacement.

One proposed solution to address the potential job displacement caused by AI is the implementation of a universal basic income (UBI). UBI is a form of social security in which all citizens or residents of a country receive a regular, unconditional payment from the government. The idea behind UBI is that it provides a safety net for workers who may lose their jobs due to automation or other factors.

Several countries have already implemented UBI pilot programs. In 2021, Spain launched a pilot program to provide a monthly payment of €625 to 1,000 families in the country. Similarly, in Finland, a two-year pilot program was launched in 2017 to provide a monthly payment of €560 to 2,000 unemployed individuals.

Proponents of UBI argue that it can provide financial security to workers who may be displaced by AI. They also argue that UBI can stimulate economic growth by providing consumers with more disposable income. In addition, UBI can help to reduce poverty and inequality, particularly for low-income households.

However, critics of UBI argue that it may disincentivize work and reduce productivity. They also argue that it may be difficult to fund a UBI program, particularly in countries with high levels of debt. In addition, some argue that UBI may not address the root causes of job displacement, and that more targeted solutions, such as retraining and upskilling programs, may be more effective.

As AI continues to be implemented in local government, there is growing concern about the potential impact on the workforce. Many jobs that involve routine, repetitive tasks such as data entry, document processing, and customer service are at risk of being automated by AI-powered tools. This could lead to job displacement for many workers.

Governments are responding to this challenge in several ways. One approach is to invest in retraining and upskilling programs for workers whose jobs are at risk of being automated. These programs can help workers transition into new roles that require higher-level skills. For example, governments could provide training in areas such as data analysis, programming, and project management. This would enable workers to adapt to the changing nature of work and acquire skills that are in high demand.

Another approach is to create new job opportunities through the implementation of AI. Governments can work with industry partners to identify areas where AI can be used to create new jobs. For example, AI could be used to develop new services or products, or to improve existing services. This would create new job opportunities for workers who are skilled in areas such as AI development, data analysis, and project management.

In addition, governments can explore the potential of new employment models such as job sharing and flexible work arrangements. Job sharing involves two or more workers sharing a single job, which can be particularly effective for jobs that require a high level of expertise. Flexible work arrangements, such as telecommuting and flexible schedules, can help workers balance work and personal responsibilities.

Finally, governments can consider the implementation of a universal basic income (UBI) to provide financial security for workers who may lose their jobs due to automation. UBI is a form of social security in which all citizens or residents of a country receive a regular, unconditional payment from the government.

The Potential Impact on the Workforce and Society

The impact of AI in IT extends beyond the field itself and can have significant implications for the workforce and society. In this section, we explore some of the potential impacts of AI on the workforce and society.

The Changing Nature of Work

As AI technology improves and becomes more prevalent, it is likely to change the nature of work. Routine tasks that are currently performed by humans may be automated, leading to a shift in the types of jobs that are available. This may require workers to develop new skills and adapt to new types of work, for instance:

- Developing AI-powered systems for citizen engagement and feedback, such as chatbots or virtual assistants, which can provide personalized assistance and support to citizens
- Using AI to analyze citizen feedback data and identify trends or patterns in citizen sentiment, which can help local governments make data-driven decisions about policy and service delivery
- Implementing AI-powered systems for public safety, such as predictive policing algorithms or emergency response systems, which can help local governments respond more quickly and effectively to threats and emergencies

As AI technology advances, it is likely that the nature of work will change significantly. Automation of routine tasks, such as data entry and basic analysis, may lead to a shift in the types of jobs that are available. This shift may require workers to develop new skills and adapt to new types of work.

According to a report by the McKinsey Global Institute, up to 375 million workers, or 14% of the global workforce, may need to change their occupations or acquire new skills by 2030 due to automation. This suggests that the impact of AI on the workforce will be significant and will require a proactive approach from both employers and employees.

However, it is important to note that not all jobs will be replaced by AI. While routine and repetitive tasks may be automated, jobs that require creativity, empathy, and critical thinking are less likely to be automated soon. In fact, some experts predict that the demand for these types of jobs may increase as AI takes over routine tasks, creating new opportunities for workers with these skills.

In addition, AI has the potential to create new jobs and industries that do not currently exist. For example, the development of

AI-powered technologies may lead to new roles in data science, machine learning, and robotics. These roles require specialized skills and knowledge that are not currently widely available in the workforce, creating new opportunities for education and training.

Furthermore, AI is also expected to create new types of jobs that require skills such as data analysis and programming. As AI systems become more advanced, there will likely be an increased demand for individuals with expertise in these areas. Additionally, as AI technology is integrated into various industries, there may be new job roles that emerge as a result. For example, AI could be used in healthcare to analyze patient data and provide personalized treatment recommendations, creating new job opportunities for individuals with both medical and technical expertise.

However, the potential displacement of human workers by AI is a major concern for many people. While some argue that AI will create new job opportunities, others fear that it will lead to widespread unemployment as machines become more capable of performing tasks that were previously done by humans. This could have significant social and economic implications, as individuals who are unable to find work may face financial hardship and reduced access to healthcare and other resources.

To address these concerns, policymakers and businesses must work together to ensure that the benefits of AI are distributed fairly and that workers are equipped with the skills needed to thrive in a changing job market. This may involve investing in education and training programs that help individuals develop skills that are in high demand, such as data analysis and programming. Additionally, businesses may need to rethink their approach to hiring and training employees, placing a greater emphasis on skills such as creativity and problem-solving that are less likely to be automated.

Overall, the changing nature of work is one of the most significant ways in which AI is expected to impact society in the coming years.

While there are certainly risks associated with this shift, there is also the potential for AI to create new opportunities and improve the lives of workers around the world. By working together to address the challenges posed by AI and to harness its potential for good, we can build a brighter future for all.

Chapter 16: The Future of Smart Government with AI

The use of artificial intelligence (AI) in local governments is growing rapidly, with governments around the world looking to leverage this technology to improve services, enhance decision-making capabilities, and create new opportunities for their workforce. In this section, we will explore the future of local governments with AI, using data from 2022 and 2023 to provide real-world examples and evidence of the impact of this technology.

Data-driven decision-making has become increasingly important in local governments as they face ever more complex challenges that require evidence-based solutions. The use of AI-powered tools is revolutionizing the way that local governments analyze and interpret data, allowing them to identify patterns and trends that might be missed by human analysts.

One of the most well-known examples of data-driven decision-making in local government is the City of Los Angeles's GeoHub, which was launched in 2016. The GeoHub is a platform that uses data analytics and mapping technology to visualize and analyze data on everything from crime rates to air quality. By analyzing this data, the city can identify patterns and trends that may not be immediately apparent to human analysts. For example, the city used the GeoHub to analyze data on traffic accidents and found that a significant number of accidents were occurring at intersections without crosswalks. This led the city to prioritize the installation of crosswalks at these intersections to improve pedestrian safety.

The GeoHub has also been used to analyze data on air quality in the city. By analyzing data from air quality sensors across the city, the GeoHub can identify areas with high levels of pollution and help the city to develop targeted interventions to improve air quality. For example, the city used the GeoHub to identify areas with high levels of diesel emissions from trucks and buses and worked with the California Air Resources Board to develop new regulations to reduce these emissions.

In addition to the GeoHub, there are numerous other examples of data-driven decision-making in local government using AI-powered tools. For example, the city of New York is using an AI-powered tool called Rapid Repairs to manage the repair and maintenance of public housing. The tool uses data analytics to identify repairs that need to be made, prioritize repairs based on their impact on tenants, and assign repair work to contractors. By using this tool, the city has been able to reduce the time it takes to complete repairs and improve tenant satisfaction.

Another example of data-driven decision-making in local government is the city of Amsterdam's CitySDK project. This project uses data analytics to develop tools that help the city to better understand and address the needs of its citizens. For example, the project developed a tool that allows citizens to report problems with streetlights using their smartphones. By using this tool, the city has been able to quickly identify and repair broken streetlights, improving safety and reducing energy consumption.

The use of AI-powered tools for data-driven decision-making in local government is not without its challenges. One of the key challenges is ensuring that the data used to train these tools is accurate and representative of the population. Biases in the data can lead to biased decision-making, perpetuating inequalities, and discrimination. Governments must also ensure that these tools are transparent and explainable, so that citizens can understand how decisions are being made.

One of the most significant trends in the use of AI in local governments is the growing focus on citizen services. AI-powered tools can help local governments provide better, more personalized services to citizens, improving satisfaction and engagement. One notable example of this is the use of AI-powered chatbots to answer citizen inquiries and provide information on a range of topics.

In the United Kingdom, the city of Manchester has implemented an AI-powered chatbot called "Buddy" to handle citizen inquiries and provide information on everything from public transportation to recycling. This chatbot is available 24/7 and can handle a wide range of inquiries, helping to reduce the workload on human customer service agents. The chatbot can also provide personalized recommendations and alerts to citizens based on their location and interests, providing a highly personalized experience.

Buddy has been highly successful, with over 50,000 interactions per month and an overall satisfaction rate of 94%. The chatbot has been particularly effective in reducing wait times for citizens, with an average response time of just 20 seconds. By using AI-powered chatbots like Buddy, local governments can provide more efficient and effective services to citizens while reducing the workload on human customer service agents.

Another example of the use of AI-powered tools for citizen services is the City of Helsinki's Digital Advisor. This tool uses natural language processing to provide personalized advice and guidance to citizens on a wide range of topics, including public transportation, healthcare, and social services. The tool can provide personalized recommendations based on a citizen's location, preferences, and needs, and can help citizens navigate complex government services more easily.

The use of AI-powered tools for citizen services is not without its challenges. One of the most significant challenges is ensuring that these tools are accessible and understandable to all citizens, including those with disabilities or limited digital literacy. Governments must also ensure that these tools are transparent and explainable, so that citizens can understand how they are making decisions and providing recommendations.

AI-powered tools are increasingly being used in local governments to improve efficiency and reduce costs. These tools can help local governments optimize a wide range of operations, from energy consumption to traffic flow.

One example of the use of AI in local government to reduce costs is the Smart Streetlight Program in the city of San Diego in the United States. The program uses sensors and AI algorithms to optimize the city's streetlights, reducing energy consumption and maintenance costs. The sensors can detect when a streetlight is not needed and turn it off automatically and can also detect when a streetlight is malfunctioning and alert maintenance crews. By using these AI-powered tools, the city has been able to reduce energy consumption by up to 60%, resulting in significant cost savings.

In addition to energy consumption, AI-powered tools can also be used to optimize traffic flow and reduce congestion. The city of Dubai in the United Arab Emirates has implemented an AI-powered traffic management system called the "Smart Traffic Management System". This system uses real-time data from sensors, cameras, and other sources to analyze traffic patterns and optimize traffic flow. The system can automatically adjust traffic signals to reduce congestion and improve safety and can provide real-time updates to drivers on traffic conditions. By using this AI-powered system, the city has been able to reduce travel time by up to 30%.

AI-powered tools are also being used in local governments to optimize a wide range of other operations, from waste management to public safety. For example, the city of Barcelona in Spain has implemented an AI-powered waste management system that uses sensors to detect when trash containers are full and need to be emptied. By using this system, the city has been able to reduce the number of waste collection trucks on the road by up to 40%, resulting in significant cost savings and reduced emissions.

While AI-powered tools can bring significant benefits to local governments in terms of efficiency and cost savings, there are also potential challenges and risks that must be addressed. One of the key challenges is ensuring that these tools are transparent and explainable, so that citizens can understand how decisions are being made. Another challenge is ensuring that these tools are used ethically and fairly, and do not perpetuate biases or discrimination.

The use of AI in local governments presents both opportunities and challenges. While AI can help local governments in making data-driven decisions and providing better services, there are significant challenges that need to be addressed. One of the key challenges is ensuring that AI is used ethically and responsibly to avoid perpetuating bias and discrimination while protecting citizen data. Governments need to ensure that AI-powered tools are transparent and explainable so that citizens can understand how decisions are being made.

One way to ensure ethical and responsible use of AI in local governments is using statistical methods to detect and mitigate potential biases. Statistical methods such as regression analysis, propensity score matching, and difference-in-differences estimation can help identify and correct biases in AI models. For example, if an AI model is used to predict recidivism rates for individuals, statistical analysis can be used to ensure that the model is not biased against certain demographic groups.

Another important consideration when using AI in local governments is the level of measurement of the data being used. Data can be measured at four hierarchical levels: nominal, ordinal, interval, and ratio. The level of measurement affects the types of statistical analysis that can be performed on the data. For example, nominal data can only be labelled and cannot be ordered or ranked, while ratio data has a true zero point and can be used to calculate meaningful ratios.

Data visualization tools can also be useful in ensuring that AI is transparent and explainable in local governments. By using visual elements such as charts and graphs, data visualization tools can help local governments present data in a way that is easy to understand for citizens. This can be particularly important when using AI in decision-making processes, as it allows citizens to see how decisions are being made and raises awareness of potential biases or inaccuracies in the data.

To provide an example of the use of AI in local governments, urban planners use statistics to make data-driven decisions on the number of apartments, shops, and stores that should be built in a certain area based on population growth patterns. AI can help streamline this process by providing more accurate predictions on future population growth. However, it is important to ensure that the AI models used in this process are free from biases that may perpetuate discrimination or inequality.

In conclusion, the use of AI in local governments presents significant challenges related to ethics, responsibility, and transparency. Statistical methods can help ensure that AI models are free from bias and discrimination, while data visualization tools can help increase transparency and explain ability. It is important for local governments to prioritize ethical and responsible use of AI to avoid perpetuating inequalities in decision-making processes.

Conclusion

This book has provided a high-level entry point into use and potential impact of artificial intelligence (AI) on the workforce and society, as well as the use of AI in local government. It explores the changing nature of work, the potential for job displacement, and the implementation of a universal basic income (UBI) as a solution. It also discusses the use of AI in citizen services, data-driven decision-making, and optimizing government operations. The challenges and risks associated with the use of AI in local governments are also addressed, including the need for transparency, ethical use, and the mitigation of potential biases. Changes are coming and there is no stopping the use of AI in our day-to-day life.

Currently it seems like the momentum is in large cities have the technical talent, venture capital, and P2P partnerships to build solution using AI. Currently, London is leading the way, second by New Your, Singapore, Washington, and Chicago. The rise of smaller boutique companies offering services to medium and small agencies is limited, but companies like Govnamics is leading the way.

About Govnamics

Are you tired of dealing with outdated government systems and sluggish decision-making processes? Are you looking for a way to revolutionize your county, local, tribal government or school district using the latest AI technologies? Then look no further than Govnamics – the AI company that specializes in all things AI for the public sector.

Our company is focused on providing innovative solutions for governments and school districts to help them operate more efficiently and effectively. We understand the unique challenges faced by the public sector, and we are committed to helping our clients overcome these challenges by leveraging the power of artificial intelligence.

With our cutting-edge AI technologies, we can help your government or school district make data-driven decisions that are both accurate and timely. Our solutions range from AI-powered traffic management systems to energy optimization in public buildings, and from optimizing school bus routes to predicting student performance.

We also offer AI-powered chatbots to improve citizen engagement and customer service, as well as facial recognition and surveillance technologies to enhance public safety. Our team of AI experts will work closely with you to understand your specific needs and tailor our solutions to meet your unique requirements.

By partnering with Govnamics, you can stay ahead of the curve and embrace the future of public sector innovation. Our goal is to help you achieve your mission and improve the lives of your citizens and students through the power of AI.

So, what are you waiting for? Contact us today to learn more about how Govnamics can help your county, local, tribal government or school district achieve its goals through AI innovation.

Don't miss out!

Visit the website below and you can sign up to receive emails whenever Chris Chiancone publishes a new book. There's no charge and no obligation.

https://books2read.com/r/B-A-LZWX-OLEIC

BOOKS 2 READ

Connecting independent readers to independent writers.

Also by Chris Chiancone

1

Smart Government: Practical Uses for Artificial Intelligence in Local Government

About the Author

Meet the versatile, top-tier, and impact-driven Chief Information Officer behind the latest tech innovation book. With over 20 years of experience, this author has been driving the development and implementation of business-led and customer-focused enterprise-level technology solutions.

Highly analytical and equipped with a combination of digital consultancy, agile frameworks, data architecture, project/program management, business analysis, QA, technical documentation, and team leadership skills, this author has what it takes to create transformative change in any organization.

In-depth experience in blending visionary insight with sharp business planning skills has enabled this author to strategize major technological change initiatives and turnaround management. From ensuring cost-effective design to implementing cutting-edge technologies, the author has executed major technology integrations and upgrades, technological transformations, and complex initiatives with unparalleled expertise.

Moreover, this author encourages innovation, out-of-the-box thinking, teamwork, and creative problem-solving. By prioritizing the implementation of cutting-edge technologies, this author is committed to supporting long-term business objectives and requirements.

The author's passion for driving change and improving outcomes is reflected in their writing, which is clear, concise, and impactful. This book is a must-read for anyone seeking to stay ahead of the curve and embrace the latest innovations in technology.

So, if you're ready to learn from a true industry expert, pick up this book and discover how you can drive transformative change in your organization today!

Read more at www.govnamics.com.

CPSIA information can be obtained
at www.ICGtesting.com
Printed in the USA
JSHW012213270423
40867JS00002B/107